Lord, Fix My Leaks!

Unleashing the Woman of God In You

CL Holley

Finding True Healing in Christ

Lord, Fix My Leaks!

Unleashing the Woman of God in You

C.L. Holley

Lord, Fix My Leaks!

Unleashing the Woman of God in You

C.L. Holley

What are women saying about this book?

"Reading this book has helped me to look at life from a different perspective and taught me how to rely on God in all circumstances. I was so blessed after reading this book; I purchased a few extra copies to bless my family and friends!" - **T. Crutcher**

"This book is ideal for answering the age old question, "Is it love?" If you've always wanted to know what it means to truly love and be loved, God's way, then this book is for you! Also, the relatable examples outlined throughout makes it easy and enjoyable for readers to relate..." – **C. Everson**

"This book has been a blessing to me in my spiritual growth, and also my church family. I see myself in many situations in the book. How can we go where God wants us to be if we don't identify where we are? An in-depth book study has been birthed out of this book, along with the word of God in our covenant friends' ministry at our church."- **E. Langford**

"I felt it was just double confirmation for me that after you get connected with the right Man-(Jesus), everything else has no choice but to line up & fall into place. Often times in the past, I found myself trying to work & figure things out on my own. I had no idea the plans God had in store for me until I let go & became completely dependent upon Him." – **T. Pitts**

Dedications

To my lovely daughter Kiana, I pray this book will cause you to long for the love of the Heavenly Father.

To all the women who ever cried out, "Lord, set me free!".

Table of Contents

Introduction   11

1: Conquering the Quiet Place   13

2: Lord, Fix My Leaks!   23

3: Lord, Make Him Love Me!   31

4: Mirror, Mirror, on the Wall   41

5: What's My Purpose?   49

6: Finding True Love   57

7: The Inner Woman   67

8: True Intimacy   77

9: Why Did He Leave Me?   87

10: My Man, My god!   97

11: Woman, Behold Your Prince!   107

12: Putting It All Together   119

13: The Essence of a Woman   135

14: The Path to Dating & Marriage   147

Introduction

As a minister and biblical counselor, I've been thoroughly blessed with the privilege of having many heart-to-heart conversations with Christian women. However, my most rewarding conversations have occurred with my daughter Kiana, who at the writing of this book recently turned eighteen.

I realize my opinion is skewed toward the daddy-loves-his-little-girl side, but she is the apple of my eye. She's a teenager blossoming into a wise young woman of God. She's blessed with charm, a witty sense of humor, honor roll intelligence, physical beauty, a sensitive conscious to right and wrong, and a vision of what she wants out of life.

There are times when I desire to stop the growing process, rewind the years, and return to the days of pretend coffee and tea, back rides on the carpet, curly pony-tailed hair, and bedtime prayers followed by tiny butterfly kisses.

I realize the attempt to rewind time is futile. Therefore, I constantly pour the word of God and myself into her life before its time for her to depart from our home and build her own life. I want her to understand certain things about herself, her relationship with a young man, and how that relationship affects her relationship with God the Father. It is with her in mind that I write this book to the daughters of God.

This book was written with a three-fold purpose. First, for women to become more intimately knowledgeable about themselves and to see beyond their external appearance. I want them to discover the beauty that lies within. Second, for women to be healed from past or present hurtful relationships with men. The actions of a man do affect a woman—sometimes in ways she never realized or imagined.

And third, to introduce to some, and present to others, Jesus Christ, in a fresh, intimate, and personal way. The purpose is to move beyond religion and into a vibrant, passionate, and fulfilling relationship with Jesus and God the Father.

I invite you to walk in the footsteps of Deborah, this book's main character, as she struggles in her times of singleness as well as her times of marriage. Follow the other characters from place to place in their life, from hurt to pain, from heartache to disappointment—but most of all, from victory to triumph, as they finally realize that not even a godly man can fill their empty void.

I have provided additional insight throughout the book into each subject matter and situation by way of the subheading *Whispers*. Whenever you come upon a *Whispers* subheading, please view it as your heavenly Father whispering words of comfort, encouragement, and counsel into your ear. I invite you to step into these pages and be forever changed.

Prayer: Father in Heaven, I pray the release of peace, comfort, and joy to every godly daughter. I ask You to meet with her in those hurtful memories and painful thoughts. I ask You to extend Your hand of healing even as she reads this book. Help them to see and experience the endless love of Jesus. I pray in the holy, graceful, and mighty name of Jesus Christ, Amen.

Chapter 1

Conquering the Quiet Place

Theme: Hidden Issues Do Affect Us.

~London 2010: Deborah speaks at an author's conference~

D eborah nervously stood backstage awaiting her introduction. According to the host, over five-thousand women filled the London auditorium. She couldn't believe all those women came just to see and hear her—an ordinary country woman from north Alabama. She could sense the excitement in the atmosphere. Minutes later the host enthusiastically announced her name.

"Ladies," the host blared, "here she is without further delay! The author who's taking the world of women by storm! She goes by the pen-name of *JC Shalom*, meaning Jesus Christ is Peace. And she will be sharing portions of her bestselling autobiography *From Pain to Promise*. Please put your hands together and show some love for Mrs. Deborah Sue Kyle!"

She barely got Deborah's name out before the crowd erupted with thunderous applauds and whistles. As she gingerly walked toward the stage, she could feel the heat of the spotlights.

When she finally stepped out into the audience's view, they instantly increased the noise. She shouted her normal greeting of *Shalom*, and again the crowd celebrated. It took several minutes to calm them, and afterwards she started her speech. She spoke about the rejection and child abuse from her father, and the sexual shame and embarrassment from her boyfriends. She shared the awful physical abuse, verbal abuse, and intimate betrayal from her two ex-husbands—detailing the deep-seated wounds and emotional trauma.

As she spoke, the reaction from some of the women revealed their hurt. Some gently wiped away tears, some buried their face in their hands as if to relive nightmares, and some affectionately embraced others to let them know they were not alone.

She always wanted to lift their spirits toward the end, so she testified about the love, comfort, and acceptance of Jesus Christ. During those moments it seemed as if a blanket of warmth hovered over the audience. As she led them in prayer, an outpouring of joyful tears served as evidence of painful walls breaking down and tumbling to the floor.

Deborah never anticipated, in her wildest dreams, that her book would land her on the largest stages in the speaking circuit. But here she was, sharing her personal relationship struggles with over five-thousand women. Everywhere she went they loved and respected her, and many wanted to be like her. But they didn't really know her.

They read about her painful struggles, but they only read the portions she wanted to share. They didn't know about the deepest of dark secrets stashed away in the far corners of her mind. They didn't realize she was partially healed and still fighting ghosts from the past. She often wondered what they would think if they knew about her hidden nightmares?

~Days Later: Deborah's trip to Phoenix, Arizona~

"Can I get you anything from the lobby while we wait on your bags?" the hostess offered. When they entered the hotel room, Deborah inspected the view from the seventh floor.

"No, thanks," Deborah replied. "I'm all right."

The hostess rolled her bags into the bedroom and continued the chat. "Did you have a good trip? I hope your travel wasn't a nightmare."

"It wasn't bad," Deborah responded—casting her purse and keys on the table. "At least I wasn't caught in the storm like so many others."

The hostess drew back the curtains and opened the blinders on the living room window. "Take a look at the awesome view," she pointed out. "The lake is so still and calm. Everything is so quiet. I think you'll enjoy the peace and quiet for the next three days."

Deborah walked over to the huge window and took in the impressive scenery below. The sun was just setting and the huge willow trees on each side of the lake gave it a sleepy appearance. The colorful flowers and roses strategically placed along the banks instilled a sense of lazy relaxation. It was beautiful and extremely calm.

"Yea," she hesitantly agreed, "it is beautiful." For most people, having peace, calm, and quiet would be ideal, but not for Deborah. She knew what problems occurred within her mind during the calm and quiet hours. She finally tore herself away from the window, flopped on the comfortable couch, kicked off her shoes, and rested her head on the armrest.

The hostess carefully made her rounds to inspect the room for the necessary needs. After expressing her contentment with the setup, she sat on the couch next to Deborah—wearing an inquisitive stare.

"Deborah," she inquired with a hint of curiosity, "can I ask you something that's rather personal?" Deborah gave her an affirming nod. She continued, "After reading your book several times, I received the impression there was something missing regarding your struggles. I can't put my finger on it, but it seems like something was omitted, perhaps on purpose. Am I correct?"

Deborah slowly inhaled, ran her fingers through her hair as she thought about the question, and gently exhaled to give herself enough time to respond. "Several people have asked that question," she said. "It must be the style of my writing or something. But I think I put it all on the pages."

The hostess peered at Deborah as if she wasn't quite convinced of her response. Even Deborah wasn't convinced. A different answer was stirring in her mind. Her inner-person was practically screaming out from the constant mental combat. Though she spoke to thousands of women about the peace and joy that arises from the midst of heartaches and pain, somehow those very elements eluded her.

"Are you sure you're going to be all right?" The hostess inquired again. "I can always come back to keep you company."

Deborah smiled and assured her, "No need to do that, I'll be fine."

"Okay," the hostess responded, making her way to the door. "I'll see you tomorrow morning for breakfast." Deborah smiled and waved. The door closed and she found herself in a familiar situation--alone, facing the quietness of her mind, and struggling with mental unconquered giants.

During another lonely and quiet night in her hotel room, the eerie haunting of a damaged past resurfaced. She couldn't bring herself to write about it—it was too painful. Now, it was beginning to take its toll emotionally and mentally.

Hours later, in the midst of the pitch-black night, she slowly sank into a dark corner of the bedroom, curled herself up in the fetal position, and prepared to meet her giants face-to-face. All the while, she allowed her mind to roam back and forth between the past and present—trying desperately to search for some similitude of peace and closure.

Chapter One Highlights

Though she spoke to thousands of women about peace and joy that arises from the midst of heartaches and pain, somehow those very elements eluded her.

There is a whole world of successful women doing incredible things in the daytime, but curled up in the fetal position in the quiet place.

For most people, having peace, calm, and quiet would be ideal, but not for her. She knew what problems occurred within her mind during the calm and quiet hours.

Chapter One Self Evaluation Questions:

Supporting Scriptures: Mat 5:23-24; Mat 6:14-15;
James 5:16

Do you have things that are hidden and need to be
confronted?

Do you have things in your life that are uncomfortable to
discuss?

Do you become defensive when others start a conversation
about certain subjects?

Do you still feel shameful, hurt, or angry over certain past
issues?

Do you avoid discussing certain subjects or situations?

I can relate to this chapter because:

Chapter 2

Lord, Fix My Leaks!

Misconception #1: I'm okay.

Theme: You can be successful in many areas of life, yet still hurting.

~Dora's story: You can't fix what you don't confront.~

The physical pain was excruciating, but Dora knew she couldn't stop. Inch by inch, foot by foot, and yard by yard, she forcefully pulled her injured body through the dessert. She was fortunate the plane crash didn't take her life, but the lives of others back at the crash site depended solely on her. After many hours of slow travel in search of help, she suddenly spotted a small oasis of water. After cooling her thirst, she thought about her family and friends at the crash site.

"I've got to get some water back to my family and friends at the plane," she uttered. But there was a problem. She had nothing to carry the water in. She visually scoured the dessert and spotted a small glass partially buried in the dirt. She furiously dug it up and immediately noticed the cracks in the glass. She had no choice but to use it. So she dipped it in the water, filling it to the brim, and began the journey back to the plane.

As she inched and stumbled back, the water leaked from several of the cracks. She tried unsuccessfully to stop the leaks with her fingers, and the sight of water hitting the ground brought groaning to her soul. Despite this, she continued, even though she knew by the time she reached the site, no water would be left. After a couple of miles all the water leaked out, and she flopped helplessly to the hot ground in frustration—weeping uncontrollably. If only the glass didn't have cracks. If she could only stop the leaks.

Just then she felt a hand nudging her. "Wake up, honey wake up," her husband Allen whispered. He continued nudging her and asked, "Honey, are you all right?" Her breathing slowed down a notch as she gained her bearings.

"Another bad dream?" Allen asked, caressing her hair. She slowly took in the view of her bedroom and realized it was all just a dream.

"Yeah, I guess so." She responded. She wiped her tears and buried her face in her hands.

"Was it the same dream? The one where you're in the plane crash?" Allen inquired.

She breathed a sigh of relief. "Yeah," She softly acknowledged. "I wish I knew what it meant. I'll be okay now," She assured him—gently kissing him on the cheek. "Let's try to get some rest. We have a long day tomorrow."

She climbed back under the covers but kept her eyes open. Allen wrapped his arms around her for comfort, but she spent the remainder of that night staring at the bedroom walls.

~Whispers~
This is a perfect picture of many women in the body of Christ. They are the glass. God is filling them with water for a thirsting and dying people. As they make their way to the people, the water is leaking from the many cracks in their lives. As a result, many are not being served and are missing out on the water.

The water signifies the many things God fills them with. The peace, joy, comfort, and patience that God fills them with is leaking out.

I'm amazed at what God is doing with women in the body of Christ. It's obvious the Lord has and will continue to position women for great and mighty things. I think the best is yet to come for them in terms of kingdom work. However, there are many women in the body of Christ who are fighting the fight of faith with vigor and passion, but carrying gigantic leaks in their lives.

Unresolved issues are leaks. Hidden issues are leaks. Put on hold issues are leaks. Ignored issues are leaks. Covered issues are leaks. Anything that takes away peace, hinders joy, and shortcuts patience is a leak. Anything that prevents intimacy from developing is a leak. My sister, just because certain things in your life are flourishing, it doesn't mean its okay.

Your business may be successful, but you're not okay. You may progress through the ranks of the company, but you are not okay. Your family may nominate you for Mother and Wife of the Year, but you're not okay. Your ministry may be flourishing, but you're not okay. When we have leaks in our lives, we are not okay. In Dora's case, the message of the dream is clear: you have unresolved issues in your life, and those issues are beginning to affect your well-being and your work for the Lord.

But there is good news. Jesus specializes in sealing cracks and leaks. So open up and don't attempt to deny your leaks for Christ is here to fill every cracked place in your life.

Prayer: Father in Heaven. I pray for every woman carrying hurtful male-made wounds in their body, soul and spirit. I pray You will touch them in the deepest and innermost portions of their hurt and release healing as a flood of waters. I pray in the name of the True Healer, Jesus Christ, Amen.

Focus: Jesus will give you peace if you give Him your problems.

Chapter Two Highlights

There are many women in the Body of Christ fighting the fight of faith with vigor and passion, but fighting with gigantic leaks in their lives.

Anything that prevents intimacy from developing is a leak. My sister, just because certain things in your life are flourishing, that doesn't mean its okay.

But there is good news. Jesus specializes in sealing the cracks and leaks. So open up and don't attempt to deny your leaks. For Christ is here to fill every cracked place in your life.

Chapter Two Self Evaluation Questions:

Supporting Scriptures: Mark 11:25-26; John 10:10;
1 John 1: 9-10

Do you feel certain things would hurt your reputation if discovered?

Are you praised in public, yet hurting in private?

Are you viewed as a "super-woman" by everyone except your family?

Do you have a problem talking about your struggles to others?

I can relate to this chapter because:

Create in me a clean heart, O God,
And renew a steadfast spirit within me.
Do not cast me away from Your presence,
And do not take Your Holy Spirit from
me. (Psalm 51:10-11)

Chapter 3

Lord, Make Him Love Me!

Misconception #2: He will love me if…

Theme: True love is beyond your control.

~Sabrina's story: The Pain of Rejection~

S abrina lay stunned and mystified in the huge empty bedroom. Only the ticks of the alarm clock broke the silence of the night. A few hours earlier her loving husband of over seven years casually dropped a total bombshell.

"Sabrina, I'm sorry," he coldly confessed, "but I just don't love you. From now on I'm going to live for me. I'll send someone for the rest of my things once I get settled." He casually walked out of their bedroom and out of her life for the last time.

His words replayed themselves like a broken record in her mind. She waited on the emotions of anger and bitterness to come, but the only thing she could feel was extreme guilt and a heavy sense of worthlessness.

She managed to muffle out thoughts of her two children. She thought things would be different after giving him the boy he always wanted. She thought surely he would learn to love her and become a committed husband and father. She wondered, What did I do wrong? Why doesn't he love me? I've done everything I can think of to make him love me.

She waited on the tears to roll down her cheeks but they never came. Instead, a cold numbness gripped her entire body as her mind drifted in and out of reality.

~Whispers~

It took Sabrina seven years to learn a valuable lesson about love. As we can see from our scriptures at the end of this chapter, Leah tried four times to win Jacob's love through giving, but never received it. In the end, she must have come to the painful conclusion: if he doesn't love me for who I am, then he won't love me for what I can give.

Sadly, there are many women in the world who are hopeful of winning the love of a man. Eventually, they all discover the following truths about real love:

1. **Real love is unconditional.**

I love you because of who you are, not what you can do or give. I will give my love without asking you for anything in return.

2. **Real love is not won, but offered without a contest.**

It is there simply because you exist. It does not attach conditions or qualifiers to its existence.

3. Giving is a response of true love, not a condition.

In other words, we give because we love. We don't give to become loved.

Consider this highly quoted scripture:

"For God so loved the world that He gave His only Begotten Son, that whosoever believes in Him should not perish, but have everlasting life." (John 3:16)

Giving was a response of God's love, not a condition. Because He loved, He gave His only begotten Son to save the world. He did not shout to the world, "If you love Me, I'll give you My Son." But He said, "I'll give you My Son because I love you."

It is proper to say, "I love you so much that I want to give you a child." But it's not proper to say, "Give me a child, and I'll love you." The latter is called conditional love.

There are hundreds of women trapped in relationships of conditional love. Perhaps the man suggests:

"If you take care of me, I'll love you."
"If you keep the weight off, I'll love you."
"If you were more like her, I'd love you."
"If you were educated, I'd love you."

All of these statements are not based on real love. They are based on conditional love. When love is conditional, the conditions are always subject to being changed. After all the conditions have been met, as in our opening story, the man is still subject to leaving because true love doesn't exist.

When a man loves you unconditionally, you won't have to worry about gaining a few pounds. When a man loves you unconditionally, you don't have to be someone else. When a man loves you unconditionally, you become free to be who you are. When a man loves you unconditionally, you don't have to worry about him falling out of love.

Therefore, I implore you to examine your relationship. Ask the man why he loves you and why he would remain with you in times of struggles. His answers should not be conditional. Even if they are, he may need to be taught what true love is.

True love must first be found in Christ. Discover how much He loves you unconditionally. Then you will have something which to compare the love of a man. My prayer for you is to find true love that erases the feelings of worthlessness and despair and fills you with the reality of never being rejected. That type of love cannot come from any human; it can only come from Jesus Christ.

~End of Whispers~

Sabrina finally shook the cobwebs out of her mind long enough to remember the words of her dying grandmother, "Sabrina, always remember who you are and whose you are. Never love anyone more than you love the Lord Jesus Christ. He loves you unconditionally."

She slowly walked into the study, found her bible that hadn't been touched in many years, and opened it to the gospel of John. As she read about the love of God found in Jesus Christ, she received a sense of acceptance and love beyond anything she ever imagined.

Prayer: My Father I pray today for the woman reading this book. I pray you will fill her with Your love, which lasts forever and never fades away. I ask You to erase her feelings of worthlessness and failure and replace them with Your peace. Let her know that she is wanted, accepted, and loved more than she could ever imagine. I pray in the name of the Man of all Men, Jesus the Christ. Amen.

Focus: Jesus loves you just because!

Chapter Three Highlights

Real love is unconditional. I love you because of who you are; not for what you can do or give. I will give my love without asking you for anything in return.

Real love is not won but offered without a contest. It is there simply because you exist. It does not attach conditions or qualifiers to its existence.

Giving is a response of true love, not a condition. In other words, we give because we love. We don't give to become loved.

Chapter Three Self Evaluation Questions:

Supporting Scriptures: Gen 29:31-32; Rom 8:39; Eph 5:25; 1John 4:7-11

Do you try hard to make others love you?

Are you terribly disappointed when others express dislike for you?

How do you react when someone doesn't return your expressions of love?

I can relate to this chapter because:

Chapter 4

Mirror, Mirror, on the Wall

Misconception #3: I am what I see.

Theme: Appearance attracts, but character keeps!

~Josephine's story: Beauty is in the eye of the beholder~

osephine brushed her long shiny hair ever so gently as she stared into the mirror at her beautiful face. As she slowly continued her morning beauty treatment, her mind faded back to the latest fight with her live-in boyfriend.

It had been a turbulent two years filled with separations, accusations, and many hurtful moments. As she looked intently on herself, for the first time in many years she was forced to look beyond her beauty and into her character.

She had used her beauty to get many things in life. She used it to get her way with boyfriends in high school and to gain material possessions from those relationships. She thought beauty was the ticket to getting everything.

But now, the words of her boyfriend seemed to shake that notion. He tearfully confessed during their latest argument, "Josephine, it hurts me to say this, but you seem to only care about yourself. I didn't realize this before we moved in together, but you are a selfish, insecure, and cold-hearted woman."

His words touched something deep within her, and at last she had to face the truth. She spent an enormous amount of time on beauty, but very little on character. As a result, she forged a trail of superficial love, love based on external appearance, in her relationships. The true love she longed for was missing. After many years, the truth hit her like a ton of bricks: Superficial love never lasts. Just as all external appearances eventually fade, so will the love on which it depends.

~Whispers~

We live in a society that heralds the message, "What you see is what you get." We are constantly tempted to believe that external appearance is everything and that our looks will get us the good life. If we have "the look," we can get an outstanding career, a corner on the Hollywood walk of fame, and the man of our dreams. The look often consists of long flowing hair, full lips, shapely thighs, and long legs, all connected to a petite body.

Some women have sought after the look so intensely and recklessly that their health has been severely damaged. It's not uncommon to hear about women being scarred and crippled for life by surgeons or techniques meant to give them "the look."

But I want you to know something fascinating about yourself. You are not the image you see in the mirror. You are much more than a picture. The most beautiful aspect about you is not your external image. It's your character.

Do you want to know what causes a man to love you deeply and unconditionally? It's not your full lips or your pear-shaped hips. It's not your long legs or your silky smooth hair. It's something hidden deep within that cannot be seen in the mirror. Simply and surprisingly, it's your character.

* It's the love and compassion you have for others.

* It's the patience you display in your everyday life.

* It's the kindness you show to complete strangers.

* It's the faithfulness and forgiveness you offer.

* It's the encouragement and inspiration you give.

* It's the complimenting words you say.

* It's the thoughtful things you do that say, "I was thinking about you today."

Therefore, learn to be forgiving and merciful. Learn to give encouraging words in the time of need. When you do these things, you will develop true love that lasts a lifetime.

When a man loves you because of these types of things, his love will never fade away. Make your greatest priority your character. Learn to be patient, kind, and thoughtful. Watch the love blossom to heights you never expected. For now, let's see how this episode in Deborah's life ends.

~End of Whispers~

Josephine's heart was ready to let go of the superficial love she built. She desired to receive the change that only Jesus could bring. She dropped her makeup, fell to her knees, and cried out to Jesus,
"Lord, create in me a clean heart, and renew within me a right spirit!"
She could sense the peace and forgiveness of Jesus surround her. Now, she truly experienced the scriptures that said, "Once in Christ we become a new creation, old things have passed away, behold, all things have become new. (2 Cor 5:17).

Prayer: Father in Heaven. I pray for all the women who are involved in superficial love relationships. I ask You to show them who they really are. Show them beauty is from the inside out. Produce within them the fruits of the Spirit that their relationships will be filled not with lust, but true love. I pray in the name of Jesus the Christ. Amen.

Focus: Beauty will get what you want, but character will keep what you get.

Chapter Four Highlights

We are constantly tempted to believe that external appearance is everything and that our looks will get us the good life. If we have the look, we can get an outstanding career, a corner on the Hollywood walk of fame, and the man of our dreams.

But I want you to know something fascinating about yourself. You are not the image you see in the mirror. You are much more than a picture.

Do you really want to know what causes a man to love you deeply and unconditionally? It's not your full lips or your pear shaped hips. It's not your long legs or your silky smooth hair. It's something hidden deep within that cannot be seen in the mirror. Simply and surprisingly, it's your character.

Chapter Four Self Evaluation Questions:

Supporting Scriptures: Pro 31:25-30; Gal 5:22-23; Col 3:8-10

How would you describe yourself to others?

Do you place more emphasis on your external or internal characteristics?

How much time daily do you spend on external verses internal values?

I can relate to this chapter because:

" Many daughters have done well,
But you excel them all.
Charm is deceitful and beauty is passing,
But a woman who fears the LORD, she
shall be praised." (Proverbs 31:29-30)

Chapter 5

What's My Purpose?

Misconception #4: He's my everything.

Theme: You have a specific God-given purpose.

~Lacy's story: Finding what God has for you~

The stone cold silence in the bedroom mesmerized Lacy. As she rolled over in bed, she found an empty spot where her husband should have been. She gazed at the clock on the nightstand. It was shortly after two in the morning.

In her heart she knew he wasn't working, but she chose to live with it. In fact, she chose to live with many hurtful things. She chose to live with his degrading comments, his self-righteous attitude, his moonlight affairs, his many lies, and his secrecy with the finances. Her only thought was, As long as he provides me with food, clothing, and a place to stay, I can manage to put up with whatever he does.

As she lay in the lonely king-sized bed, she realized something about herself. She had made him the center of her world and the sole source of her life. Somehow she lost her identity and failed to develop her talents and gifts. Now she found herself totally dependent on a man who didn't love her.

~Whispers~

Many women make the same mistake as Lacy after they say, "I do." They become so absorbed in the lives of the man or children that they fail to develop and utilize their gifts and talents. As a result, they end up living only to support another person's life and calling.

When this happens, there is a huge sense of dependency for that person. It may even reach the point where she may tolerate being abused or misused. She doesn't think she has what it takes to survive on her own. Instead of uniting and forming one relationship, she has become absorbed into another person's life. She exists solely for him or the children.

It is customary in most countries and particularly in America for the woman to take the last name of the man in marriage. This officially identifies her with him. But in recent years more women have begun to include their maiden name with their married name. This indicates their desire to keep their identity as they enter into the relationship.

This is not an act of defiance nor is it necessary to give up one's God-given identity. In fact, it demonstrates what God has already set forth in the scriptures, that the husband and wife shall become one flesh. This doesn't mean her gifts become his gifts, or her talents become his talents, or her calling becomes his calling. She is still a unique person called to form one relationship.

Therefore she needs something in her life that allows her to exercise her gifts, talents, callings, and makes her the ultimate responsible party for its outcome. She needs something she can own.

Please don't misunderstand my point. Serving others is a good thing. In fact, the Bible teaches us to serve one another. There is nothing wrong with serving and assisting husbands or children. There is nothing wrong with co-laboring with the man to achieve great things for God. However, there should be an area in her life that is reserved just for her.

A sure test of a completely self-absorbed person is to identify something in her life that belongs solely to her. Many women cannot. Everything they're associated with belongs to their husband or children. They have nothing to call their own.

My suggestion for those is to first discover their gifts and talents. If there is a problem doing this, answer these two questions:

1. What do I like doing?
2. What am I good at?

These answers will lead you to your gifts and talents. Use your answers from the two questions to start your own pet project. For example, if you named organizing or managing, start a pet project or even small business that allows you to utilize those talents.

Whatever you do, do it in the name and to the glory of God and He will bless you tremendously. Your life will be filled with excitement and anticipation as Lacy discovered at the end of this episode in her life.

~End of Whispers~

The thoughts of insecurity preoccupied Lacy's mind. She slowly rolled out of bed and picked up a book she hadn't read in many years—the Holy Bible. She turned to the last place bookmarked and read these words:

"Moreover whom He predestined, these He also called; whom He called, these He also justified; and whom He justified, these He also glorified." (Romans 8:29)

She suddenly realized what she had to do. She had to seek God and find His plan for her life. She prayed, "Lord, help me to develop the talents and gifts You have given me." As she continued to read, the fear and anxiety that previously gripped her slowly disappeared, and the excitement of discovering what God had for her was overwhelming.

Prayer: Father in Heaven I pray that You help each of Your daughters to see and fulfill their godly calling. Help them to develop the talents and gifts You have given them. Father, teach them to soar high and accomplish mighty deeds for the Kingdom. I pray in the name of Jesus the Christ. Amen.

Focus: Your godly calling doesn't end when you say, "I do."

Chapter Five Highlights

Many women make the same mistake as Lacy after they say, "I do." They become so absorbed in the lives of the man or children that they fail to develop and utilize their gifts and talents. As a result, they end up living only to support another person's life and calling.

Therefore she needs something in her life that allows her to exercise her gifts, talents, callings, and makes her the ultimate responsible party for its outcome. She needs something she can own.

Whatever you do, do it in the name and to the glory of God and He will bless you tremendously. Your life will be filled with excitement and anticipation.

Chapter Five Self Evaluation Questions:

Supporting Scriptures: Jer 1:4-5; Rom 8:29; Phil 1:6; Col 1:9-10

Do you know what your gifts and talents are?

What do you think you are called to do?

At the moment, are you absorbed into another person's life?

I can relate to this chapter because:

"For everyone to whom much is given, from him much will be required; and to whom much has been committed, of him they will ask the more." (Luke 12:48)

Chapter 6

Finding True Love

Misconception #5: Materialism equals love?

Theme: Materialism is not proof of love.

~Ambrosa's story: The love of things~

Ambrosa yelled to her husband as she breezed through the living room. "Hurry up Marcus! We don't want to be late for our lunch with Maria!"

"I'm coming, I'm coming!" Marcus responded. He dipped down the stairs, flinging a tie around his neck. "I don't see why this lunch date is so important to you anyway. She's just your old friend from college whom you haven't seen in over twenty years. So what if she's married to a rich oil executive? She's not the Queen of England."

"You don't understand," Ambrosa quickly retorted. "Maria and I were best friends. We talked about everything and shared everything, including our life's dreams. We both wanted to marry a successful man and live a life of luxury. I simply wanted to show her that my dream has also come true."

Marcus gazed at her—his face formed tiny wrinkles of curiosity. "Ambrosa, am I just a status symbol?" He asked.

She brushed the question aside, "Oh Marcus, don't be silly. You know I love you." She straightened his tie and kissed him on the cheek, and they headed toward the car.

They buckled into their brand new Bentley and Ambrosa gazed at their multi-million-dollar home through the rear view mirror. As they drove off she thought, I can't wait to see Maria and show off my CEO husband and all of the trimmings.

They arrived at the restaurant a bit early and took a seat next to the window. Ambrosa impatiently peered into the streets, waiting to catch the first glimpse of Maria. She saw a woman who looked somewhat like Maria, but decided it couldn't be.

The couple drove up in a simple car and their dress was very modest, unlike the woman Ambrosa knew. When the couple entered the restaurant, Ambrosa realized it was indeed Maria. But the man she was with was not her husband.

"Ambrosa!" Maria squealed as she made her way to their table. "It's great to see you after all these years!" They affectionately embraced, then turned to introduce their men.

"Maria, this is my husband Marcus," Ambrosa bragged. "He is the CEO of the fasting-growing company in our state."

"Really!" Maria gasped, "that must be exciting!" Maria affectionately took the hand of her companion and happily announced, "And this is my husband Michael. We've been married now for over three years and they have been three of the best years of my life." Maria snuggled next to Michael and he gently kissed her on the cheek.

Attempting to deal with the shock, Ambrosa grabbed Maria by the hand and suggested, "Let's go to the powder room while the men get acquainted." She whisked her away to the bathroom. As they powdered their faces and talked about old times, Ambrosa couldn't help but pry a little about Maria's ex-husband.

"So, ah, I hate to poke in your personal life," Ambrosa said, "but what happened to the rich oil executive?"

Maria hesitated, "Oh that—well—it's a long story but I'll make it short. I realized our marriage wasn't for the right reason. I didn't love him and he didn't love me. We were just business partners enjoying a luxurious lifestyle. A few years after our divorce, I met Michael and he introduced me to Christ. Now the two most important men in my life are Jesus and Michael. They both truly love me and it's overwhelming at times."

As the evening continued, Ambrosa noticed something different about the attitude of her old friend. In fact, Maria's entire conversation was different. She no longer talked about things or accomplishments. She talked about relationships and special moments with Jesus and Michael. She seemed to beam with joy, and the way they looked at each other resembled a picture on the cover of a romance novel.

Ambrosa's eyes rested on her thousand-dollar watch, three-carat gold ring, and finally on her husband Marcus. She suddenly realized what their relationship was missing. It was missing true love.

~Whispers~

There are many women who see life as Ambrosa saw it. For them, love cannot be attained without materialism. Somehow, at least in their minds, they have mistakenly confused materialism with love. Perhaps their viewpoint was shaped as a child or as a teen.

At some point in their lives they began to say, "Shower me with your love: with the house of my dreams, with the car that's the envy of all my friends, with the closet filled with the finest of clothes, and with the dream vacations around the world."

As of the writing of this book, the decline in the U.S. housing market has left thousands of previously wealthy people without homes. Foreclosures are estimated to be over one million and the decline in the job market has left many jobless. I can only imagine how many people who where living the good life are now living below the poverty level.

I wonder how many marriages survived the loss of the house, the loss of the car, the loss of the expensive clothing, the loss of income, and the access to anything they wanted anytime they wanted it. I wonder how many wives told their husbands, "I can't live like this. I'm not accustomed to this lifestyle. I know you are trying hard and I'm sorry. But I want a divorce." Jesus warned a crowd of people when a jealous man complained about his brother's inheritance, "Take heed and beware of covetousness, for one's life does not consist in the abundance of the things he possesses." (Luke 12:15)

To summarize the scripture; life is not about things. We need to be very careful not to allow things to have control of us. In fact, there should not be any connection between love and materialism. Materialism is here one day and gone the next. However, true love is here today and in spite of what occurs tomorrow, remains present.

Eventually, all materialistic women discover the truth about love. As Ambrosa witnessed her old friend's true love, she figured out how Maria could leave an oil executive with the extravagant lifestyle, and live happily in an ordinary lifestyle

60

with an ordinary man. Her answer was simple: true love is not about stuff."

Prayer: Our Father in Heaven I pray for the thousands of women who are in Ambrosa's seat. Show them that a life of love is not about materialism or status symbols, but about relationships with true love. I pray You will show them what true love is through Your Son Jesus the Christ. In His name, I pray. Amen.

Focus: Materialism cannot hold you, comfort you, gently kiss you goodnight, or look into your eyes with longing and say, "I love you."

Chapter Six Highlights

There are many women who see life as Ambrosa saw it. For them, love cannot be attained without materialism. Somehow, at least in their minds, they have mistakenly confused materialism with love.

I wonder how many marriages survived the loss of the house, the loss of the car, the loss of the expensive clothing, the loss of income and the access to anything they wanted anytime they wanted it.

In fact, there should not be any connection between love and materialism. Materialism is here one day and gone the next. However, true love is here today and in spite of what occurs tomorrow, remains present.

Chapter Six Self Evaluation Questions:

Supporting Scriptures: Ecc 6:9; Luke 12:13-15; Phil 4:11-13; Heb 13:5

Are you Materialistic? Take this small test to see. You must be honest!

1. Do you get an attitude when you don't get the things you want?
2. Do you tend to try and keep up with the Jones?
3. Do you only have friends that reflect your lifestyle?
4. Does the loss of or acquiring of things cause you to be happy or sad?
5. Do you sin or risk things and relationships to get materialism?

I can relate to this chapter because:

Chapter 7

The Inner Woman

Misconception #6: All men are dogs.

Theme: All men are not alike.

~Jessica's story: The cold-hearted woman~

The newly hired co-worker slowly made his way toward Jessica's desk. She continued to shuffle papers and watched him out of the corner of her eye. Great, she complained within herself, we need another man around here like we need another bad stock report. Aren't there enough of those around here already?

Her life had been stormy in regards to men. Time after time they seemed to break her heart after she fell in love with them. She was an intelligent, witty, and beautiful young woman. In spite of this, her first real love hurt and embarrassed her by failing to show up for her storybook wedding. That was the last straw. From that point on she vowed to make war with every man she met.

She noticed Jeremy was a handsome young man without a wedding ring. As he made his way around to meet everyone, he finally arrived at her desk.

"Excuse me," he softly spoke—extending his hand, "my name is Jeremy. I'm your new co-worker. How are you doing?"

Jessica continued to read papers, never even looking up at him, and certainly not meeting his hand gesture. She managed to squeeze out a cold, "I'm fine. It's nice to meet you."

Jeremy slowly withdrew his hand and exited her cube. She chuckled, thinking how much fun she was going to have while destroying him. He seemed to be so gullible.

After months of being around him, she noticed something unique about his character. He didn't seem like any of the guys she previously dated. He had the utmost respect for her and often encouraged her business ideas.

Still, she was intent on making him beg like the rest of them. She found the perfect opportunity to corner him as they relaxed in the break room after a late evening meeting.

Time to put my plan into action, she schemed. She slowly took her hair down, arranged it beautifully, leaned over close to Jeremy, and seductively asked, "Jeremy, do you think I'm attractive?"

Jeremy didn't give an immediate answer. In fact he took another drink of coffee as she awaited his response. Instead of bursting out the usual response of, "Yes, I think you're very attractive," Jeremy asked an unusual question. "In what way Jessica?" He slowly took another sip of coffee as she struggled with an answer. His question puzzled her.

Jeremy continued, "The things that attract me to a woman are her characteristics, like patience, warmth, compassion, kindness, and forgiveness. She must be able to forgive others for the wrongs committed against her."

She was so embarrassed. She could literally feel her face flush. By the look on his face, she could imagine he plainly saw it as well.

Jeremy asked, "Jessica, when you look into the mirror, what do you see?"

She thought for a moment and avoided a response. She slowly rose from her seat and whispered, "I have some things I need to finish."

Jessica made her way to the desk and pulled out a small mirror. As she gazed into it, she saw a woman filled with hurt and hate. She decided to do something she hadn't done in many years. She prayed, "Lord, clean me from the inside out. Help me to have all those things Jeremy mentioned and more.

~Whispers~

Jessica had a flaw in her eyesight. She didn't see men as individuals, but as grouped in the same category. To her, whatever one man did, eventually all men would do. She allowed her past experiences with a few men to dictate her future with all men.

There are thousands of women, even spiritual women, who are carrying wounds and huge chips on their shoulders from past relationships. They are attributing these chips to every future man they meet. Because of this, some women have vowed to live without a man for the rest of their lives—not out of commitment toward God, but out of bitterness toward men.

I believe the Samaritan woman whom Jesus met at the well labeled men as "dogs" and "hopeless disappointments." The woman had endured five failed marriages and ended up in an affair with the sixth man (John 4:17-18). I also believe, after she met Jesus, she knew He was vastly different from any of the six men she previously given herself to.

Jesus not only knew about her hurtful past, He also knew what she desired. Jesus knew she hadn't completely given up on one particular man, for she mentioned the coming Messiah (Savior)—the Man she was awaiting. In making this statement, I believe she revealed the hope that one man was still out there somewhere. That man would be all she ever wanted and more.

I don't think her thirst was for mere physical water. I believe her thirst was for a relationship with true love, commitment, acceptance, and warmth. So when Jesus announced, "I am the Man you are waiting for," she dropped her water pot and ran into town telling everyone about Jesus. I believe He met her every emotional and spiritual need without any physical contact.

It would seem she finally found the right man, after about seven relationships, who completely fulfilled her desires. However, there are women who give up trying after a few disappointments.

There is also the aspect of bringing baggage from a previous relationship into the present relationship. Some women can't seem to separate one relationship from another and end up looking and listening for the patterns of previous hurts. This results in their inability to create a meaningful, trustworthy, and intimate bond with their present godly man.

The result is a woman who can't trust, can't believe in, can't become intimate with, and can't love her present godly man because she sees him exactly like her previous ungodly man. She lives in expectation that someday he will betray her trust, for she thinks, It's just a matter of time before he does the same thing.

For all of the women who have gone through difficult relationships and have finally found their Prince Charming, I praise God and celebrate with you. For the women who have decided to remain celibate because they want to give themselves totally to the Lord, I salute your decision and pray for your strength in the Lord.

For the women who are still awaiting their Prince Charming, I say, "Wait on the Lord and be patient with Him." For the women whose storms, scars, wounds, and heartaches have led them to hate all men, I pray the Lord will heal, comfort, and lead your heart in a different direction. I ask the Lord to send the chosen man into your life. How do you know when your Prince Charming arrives?

* When your heart leaps with excitement at the sound of his voice.
* When he loves you regardless of your past and present sins.
* When he encourages and supports you to be all you can be for God.
* When you feel the need to tell others about him.

First, you may need to follow Jessica's example in the story. You may need to look deeply into the mirror, confess your hurt, and ask Jesus to create in you a clean heart and renew within you a right spirit.

Prayer: Our Father in heaven. We speak to all of the hurting women today. We speak to those who have been mistreated, abused, and unloved by men. Father, please help them not to become bitter and filled with anger, but to forgive and develop the qualities You want them to have. I pray in the name of Jesus the Christ. Amen.

Focus: Ask the Lord to help you see beyond the exterior and into the hearts of men.

Chapter Seven Highlights

Jessica had a flaw in her eyesight. She didn't see men as individuals, but as grouped in the same category. To her, whatever one man did, eventually all men would do.

...some woman have vowed to live without a man for the rest of their lives, not out of commitment toward God, but out of bitterness toward men.

You may need to look deeply into the mirror, confess your hurt, and ask Jesus to create in you a clean heart and renew within you a right spirit.

Chapter Seven Self Evaluation Questions:

Supporting Scriptures: 1Sam 16:7; Mat 5:22; Col 3:12-14

Do you carry a grudge against men?

Do you think you can trust a man?

When hurt by a man, do you tend to hold it against the next man?

I can relate to this chapter because:

Chapter 8

Finding True Intimacy

Misconception #7: Intimacy equals sex.

Theme: True intimacy goes beyond the bedroom.

~Jennifer's story: The path to true intimacy~

Stephen and Jennifer cuddled at their newly renovated beach home in Florida under a spectacular view of the sunset.

"Jennifer, can you believe it's been over ten years?" Stephen inquired.

She snuggled closer, gazed into his eyes, and whispered, "I wish this moment could last forever."

As they continued relaxing and basking in the moment, her mind wandered back to her past stormy relationships that all ended in tragedy. Now, in the pleasure of this moment, she understood why.

She lost her mother at an early age and was never close to her alcoholic father. All her life she desperately searched for warmth, acceptance, and love. She thought it could only be found through physical relationships with men but she was wrong.

At last she found a godly man in Stephen. Their years of marriage were not without storms. Their relationship endured severe sickness, lost of occupations, challenges with their children, and challenges with each other. But through it all, they still clung tightly to one another.

Through the trials they gained a deeper knowledge of each other, which in turn led to a deeper appreciation and a higher valuing of each other.

She thought how wonderful it was to be in the arms of a man who loved her in spite of her past, who appreciated her for who she was, and who will never leave her no matter what.

As Stephen gently kissed her, she thanked God in her inner most being with the words, "I thank You Lord for showing me what true intimacy really is."

~Whispers~

It took some searching, but Jennifer finally discovered the path to true intimacy. It wasn't found in sexual relationships. It was forged through the heartaches and pain of becoming "one."

Sadly, many couples never find true intimacy in their relationship. When the trials, heartaches, pains, and challenges surface, they choose to break the relationship instead of breaking themselves through humility.

What is your definition of intimacy? Most women would define it as sexual relations. While this would be partially correct, intimacy goes far beyond the events of the bedroom. I want to challenge your thinking by sharing three key elements of true intimacy.

Element #1: Love

The first element is Love. There must be love in the relationship in order for true intimacy to exist. In fact, in terms of the bedroom, most women mistake love for lust. Let's do a side-by-side comparison of love and lust.

* Love focuses on giving. Lust focuses on taking.

* Love says, "I want to give myself to you." Lust says, "I want to take you and fulfill my desires."

* Love is satisfied with who you are. Lust is never satisfied and requires constant change.

Because lust is totally focused on the external person, it often becomes bored with seeing the same eyes, hair, and body. In order for it to remain interested, it demands that you become someone else. Perhaps you may go from blonde to redhead, from blue eyes to green, from short to tall.

It may even require you to change occupations in order to "spice up" the relationship. It will cast you in the role of a police officer one night, complete with handcuffs and nightstick, and the next night as a prostitute on the street corner looking for a good time.

On the other hand, love will be completely satisfied with seeing the same person, the same way, each and every night. Why? Because love sees beyond the physical person and into their journey in life together.

When love looks at you, it sees the ups and downs, the good and bad, the struggles and trials. It appreciates the fact that after all you've been through together, you still desire to be there at that given moment. Therefore love is thrilled just to hold you, to hear your voice, to listen to your heartbeat, to see your face, and feel your breath.

Please don't misunderstand. There is nothing wrong with making changes in your appearance in order to remain attractive. However, when the change becomes so drastic that it causes the man to think of someone else while with you, then it becomes lust.

Therefore be very careful about what goes on in the bedroom and in the relationship. Make sure the glue that holds your relationship together is love, not lust.

Element #2: Acceptance

Everyone wants to be loved and wanted by someone. The desire to be accepted is so powerful that some women often do ill-advised things to gain acceptance from men. Some women give their bodies prematurely. Others give up their careers or even their calling. But a man should accept you without requiring anything in return.

Keep in mind that whenever your acceptance requires a condition, it's not true acceptance. When a man knows about your past but chooses not to hold it against you, that's true acceptance. When he doesn't allow where you've been or what you've done to affect his love for you—that's true acceptance.

Where there is true acceptance, there is no need to hide things, to cover up situations, or to lie about the past, present, or future. You are free to be open and honest, not fearing rejection. This is what Jennifer finally found with Stephen.

Element #3: Commitment

Commitment can be defined as a promise to be there no matter the situation. In other words, I can count on you in the thick and thin, in the ups and downs, and in the good and bad.

When a woman has a committed man, she doesn't worry about what the future holds. She knows no matter what they face tomorrow, they will face it together. She has the confidence and assurance that through sickness, disease, financial woes, or any other trial or tribulation, her man will always be there for her.

If she falls ill, she can count on him to step into the role of "Mister Mom." She can count on him to prepare the table, care for the kids, clean the house, and look lovingly into her eyes as she helplessly lays on the sick bed, and say, "You're so beautiful," even though she knows she doesn't look how she normally does.

Commitment is all too often lacking in many relationships today. But when it's present, it causes intimacy to flourish like a flower. The man and woman in the relationship will never grow tired or weary of each other. They only look forward to facing life together.

These are the three elements of true intimacy. Now it's time to put your relationship to the test. Do you have these elements present? If not, ask the Lord to help you both develop true intimacy and follow His lead.

Prayer: Father in Heaven. There are so many women among Your daughters searching for true intimacy. I pray You would shower them with Your love, acceptance, and commitment. Amen.

Focus: First comes trials, then deeper knowledge, then deeper appreciation, then intimacy.

Chapter Eight Highlights

The first element is Love. There must be love in the relationship in order for true intimacy to exist. In fact, in terms of the bedroom, some women mistake love for lust.

Everyone wants to be loved and wanted by someone. The desire to be accepted is so powerful that some women often do ill-advised things to gain acceptance from men.

Commitment can be defined as a promise to be there no matter what the situation may be. In other words, I can count on you in the thick and thin, in the ups and downs, and in the good and bad.

Chapter Eight Self Evaluation Questions:

Supporting Scriptures: 1 Cor 13:4-7; Rom 8:38

Do you tend to think of intimacy as sex only?

What types of things do you consider intimate besides sex?

Write down some intimate things you have shared or done with a man?

I can relate to this chapter because:

Chapter 9

Why Did He Leave Me?

Misconception #8: Something's wrong with me.

Theme: Your worth is not determined by others.

~Veronica's story: The hurt of abandonment~

Veronica clutched the foreclosure notice tightly as she read it for the third time. The only emotion she experienced was fear. What am I going to do now? She pondered. At five o'clock in the morning, she sat motionless on the couch and wondered about her small daughter. How was she going to take care of her?

Then anger escaped her lips as she screamed, "How could he do this to me! He knows I can't provide for us both on my income alone! He's the lowest of the low and I hope he gets everything that's coming to him!" She broke down in tears.

Her husband decided he no longer wanted any part of the married life. He took his belongings, along with the money in their bank account, and disappeared into thin air. Three months ago she came home from work and found the house half empty and their bank account drained.

Here she was in a strange city with no friends—having left family thousands of miles away. She tried to figure out what she was going to do. Feelings of rejection and abandonment resurfaced as she wept bitterly. She slowly wiped her tears and entertained some questions:

"What did I do wrong?"

"Why did he leave me?"

This wasn't the first time she asked these questions. As a little girl, her father was in and out of her life. Even when he was there, he didn't seem interested in spending time with her. She could remember trying so hard to get his attention and approval but always came up short.

As a result, she grew up with the haunting idea: Maybe if I were a boy, he would love me and want me. A huge hole was left in her heart from her father's rejection, and this incident caused it to re-open.

That's not all. She thought back to her first crush in high school. Her boyfriend was handsome, intelligent, and could choose any girl he wanted. He chose her. After a few months of dating, he dumped her. She tried all she knew to keep him, but she finally decided to accept the hurt after he callously told her, "I don't love you and I don't want you anymore."

Those words seemed to grind her heart into powder as she wrestled with the question, What's wrong with me?

As she recalled these hurtful incidents, she came to the painful conclusion that there was something about her that needed changing but she couldn't figure out what.

~Whispers~

There are many women who have walked in Veronica's shoes. Being neglected, rejected, and abandoned can cause people to doubt themselves or become dissatisfied with who they are. To be neglected means to be overlooked. The person may be physically there but fails to share valuable time.

Abandonment means to leave someone alone with no or very little means to provide for themselves. To be rejected and unwanted, is one of the worst feelings one can ever experience and can lead to low self-esteem. One of the first reactions is to think of something we can change about ourselves in order to be accepted by others.

The typical divorce often contains all of these emotions and more. The woman feels neglected, which leads to a rift in the relationship. She feels rejected when the man says, "I want out." She feels abandoned because she's often left in a financial strait, usually with children. But I want to share a few things with you in case you are having doubts about yourself.

> You are lovable.

We all have faults, hang-ups, and sins. At the same time we also have qualities that others can fall in love with. When a man fails to fall in love with you, it's simply because he is blind and cannot see past your faults and into your lovable qualities.

Therefore, stop crying over blind men who cannot see your true beauty. Instead, pick your head up, wipe your tears, and focus first and foremost on your relationship with Christ, and everything else will fall into place.

> You are who you are.

Don't try to change who you are to make a man fall for you. Always be who you are. Talk the way you talk, behave the way you behave, respond the way you respond, and react the way you react. If a man doesn't love you for who you are, he won't love you for who you try to become. Remember, true love cannot be won, it's there simply because.

> You are wanted.

Don't become discouraged or down on yourself and don't see yourself as external only. If you want to share your life with a godly man, there is a Prince looking for the qualities you possess. He's searching for someone with your faithfulness, your patience, your smile, your sense of humor, your strength, your intelligence, and your love for Christ. You must be patient and focus on coming closer to Christ and not the time lapse between the years.

> You can make it.

If it were necessary, you could make it with your own mind, your own occupation, and your own intelligence. I'm convinced that when the chips are down, no one becomes more creative than a woman. My mother is my inspiration in this area.

My father's sudden death left her with nine children. She had an eighth-grade education and no work skills, but she found a way to feed and clothe all of us. She never remarried but she still found peace and joy. She is a living testimony that when you fully rely on Christ, all things are possible.

Someone should share these points with Veronica and all women like her. I'm sure you know of a person somewhere, or perhaps you can identify with her feelings of insecurity and fear. She needs to know she hasn't even scratched the surface of the potential God placed in her. If she would only commit herself to Him and trust Him, she would see things happen in her life that would surpass all understanding. That fact is not just true for Veronica; it's also true for you.

Prayer: My Father in Heaven, I speak Your word to every doubting and insecure woman reading this book. I pray Your word will instill confidence and security deep within her soul. Let her know she can be all she wants to be in You. I pray in the name of Jesus Christ. Amen.

Focus: When you put a man's word above God, you've made that man a god.

Chapter Nine Highlights

Being neglected, rejected, and abandoned can cause people to doubt themselves or become dissatisfied with who they are.

We all have faults, hang-ups, and sins. At the same time we also have qualities that others can fall in love with.

Don't try to change who you are to make a man fall for you. Always be who you are. Talk the way you talk, behave the way you behave, respond the way you respond, and react the way you react.

Chapter Nine Self Evaluation Questions:

Supporting Scriptures: Genesis 21:14-16; Psalms 27:10; John 1:10-11, 16:32-33

How would you rate your overall godly self-esteem: high, medium, or low?

Do you tend to blame yourself when others treat you wrong?

Do you think you are lovable and that you would be a good match for someone if you wanted someone in your life?

I can relate to this chapter because:

Chapter 10

My Man, My god!

Misconception #9: I worship the ground he walks on.

Theme: God's word should be your standard.

~Lydia's story: Putting man in his proper place~

The entire room violently trembled when he slammed the bedroom door. Lydia hated nights like this, and lately there had been plenty of them. She could always tell when her boyfriend was having one of those days. First he would begin to complain about any and everything, including her. When she attempted to make changes, he often became angry, loud, and verbally abusive.

His numbing words penetrated her soul and lodged themselves in her head. "Lydia, you were nothing when I found you and took you in!" he scolded. "Nobody else wanted you and no one would even touch you! Look at yourself! You're a high school dropout and an ex-convict! Who in their right mind would want you? I'm all you have and without me you would still be wasting away on the streets!"

Lydia spent most of her childhood in and out of foster care due to the death of her parents and no relatives. She decided to leave her last foster family at age fifteen and make the streets her home. she soon fell into prostitution, drug use, and petty crimes. That's when she met her boyfriend. He seemed friendly enough, and she just wanted someone, anyone, to take her in.

She was grateful for what he did, but he never allowed her to forget it. In fact, he seemed to establish his superiority over her and consistently reinforced the idea that she had to have him in order to live.

When she first heard his words years ago, she held out hope that things would get better. she tried any and everything to satisfy him, but still there were explosions.

She uncurled herself from the corner of the bed and walked slowly toward the mirror. As she gazed at her image, she finally accepted his hurtful words. "He's right," She whispered. "Look at me. Nobody wants me. He's all I have. I just have to try harder to make him happy."

~Whispers~

Thousands of women can identify with where Lydia is and with how she feels. Isn't it strange how a person can hear something they know isn't true the first time and brush it off, yet after hearing it over and over, can start to believe it? Here is a word of warning. Anytime you believe a man's words over those of God, you have just created an idol and effectively turned him into a god.

When a man's untrue words begin to rob you of your dignity, you think too highly of him. When what he does or says makes you think you're nothing or unworthy, you think too highly of him. When you think you can't live without him, you think too highly of him. And when you accept his words over God's word, you certainly think too highly of him.

Let's explore some things the Word of God says about you.

1. "I will praise You, for I am fearfully and wonderfully made." (Psalms 139:14)

You are not a mistake! Perhaps your childhood or other relationships were filled with hurtful memories and pain, but God saw you before your birth and knew everything that would happen in your life. Some things He prevented, others He allowed. Sometimes we wish some things in our lives never happened, but they did. This doesn't mean God wasn't there or didn't care. It just means He allowed it for a greater purpose.

2. "He who finds a wife finds a good thing and obtains favor from the Lord." (Proverbs 18:22)

You are a "good thing" and you bring favor into the life of a man. When a man finds you, his life and relationship with God should improve. Every relationship has its ups and downs, but overall there should be more good times than bad. Your man should be able to say without hesitation, "I'm better off to have found her, and now I've grown closer to God because of her."

3. "Death and life are in the power of the tongue, and those who love it will eat its fruit." (Proverbs 18:21)

There is power in what you say. Jesus said, "Out of the abundance of the heart, the mouth speaks." What's on our minds will eventually come out of our mouths. What others say about us can hurt, but what really matters is what we say about ourselves. If you have a negative view of yourself or low self-esteem, start saying good things about yourself and your mindset will improve.

4.   "Her children rise up and call her blessed; Her husband also, and he praises her." (Proverbs 31:28)

Your children and man should bless and praise you. All families have their challenges, but they should have a positive report about you to others. The neighbors, family, and friends should hear their praises for you and know you are truly blessed.

5.   "For whom He foreknew, He also predestined to be conformed to the image of His Son." (Romans 8:29)

You have a God-given purpose for this life. Sometimes you may feel as if your life doesn't matter, but it does. God has predetermined your destiny. All you have to do is seek Him with all your heart and soul.

6.   "Therefore, if anyone is in Christ, he is a new creation; old things have passed away, behold, all things have become new." (2 Corinthians 5:17)

In Christ, your past doesn't matter. He doesn't hold anything against you like others tend to do. You are a new person, ready to discover what God has for you. Do not allow others to tag you with your past. Your future with Christ will be exciting and challenging. With Christ, it doesn't matter where you started, only where you end.

7.   "Yet in all these things we are more than conquerors through Him who loved us." (Romans 8:37)

No matter what challenges or disappointments you face, you will overcome. Because of the love of Christ, the fight has already been won. Will there be disappointments? Yes. Will there be heartaches? Yes. But in spite of all this, you will end up on the winning side. You will conquer the enemy, your sins, your nightmares, and your shortcomings. And you will reign with Christ forever!

If God loves you this much, how can any man say you are nothing, unworthy, unlovable, and unwanted? Who are you going to believe, him or God? It certainly hurts when someone you care about belittles or degrades you, but you should always chase away the hurt with the truth of God.

Therefore, stand on God's word about yourself and never shed another heartbroken tear over a man's words. After all, it's not what he says that matters, it's what you say and believe that counts.

~End of Whispers~

As Lydia fixed her eyes on the mirror, she noticed a small book laying on the nightstand behind her. She slowly turned around, walked over to the nightstand, and picked it up. The book was a gift, given to her a few weeks ago by a Christian friend. She had never opened the book.

The words *The Holy Bible* were written on the cover. She opened it and found a handwritten note from her friend saying, "Please read the scriptures in Psalms 139. They will show you how much God loves and cares about you. Read them as though God is talking directly to you."

As she read those scriptures, she felt a sense of love, respect, and desire for her that she had never felt from anyone. She continued to bathe in the words as they slowly restored her sense of worth.

Prayer: Lord God, I pray for all the women who have been told ungodly things about themselves. Let them know they are more precious than silver or gold. Hold them tightly during their midnight moments and bring them into a place of refreshment and confidence in You. I pray in the name of Jesus Christ. Amen.

Focus: What others say can hurt, but what you say can cause severe damage to your soul.

Chapter Ten Highlights

Anytime you believe a man's words over those of God, you have just created an idol and effectively turned him into a god.

When you think you can't live without him, you think too highly of him. And when you accept his words over God's word, you certainly think too highly of him.

If God loves you this much, how can any man say you are nothing, unworthy, unlovable, and unwanted? Who are you going to believe, him or God?

Chapter Ten Self Evaluation Questions:

Supporting Scriptures: Exodus 20:1-2; Matthew 10:37-39; Hebrews 4:12-13

Do you have problems deciding issues without another person's input?

Does what others say about you cause you to make a change to please them?

Do another person's words hurt you to the point of going into depression?

I can relate to this chapter because:

"yet for us there is one God, the Father, of whom are all things, and we for Him; and one Lord Jesus Christ, through whom are all things, and through whom we live."
(1Corinthians 8:6)

Chapter 11

Woman, Behold Your Prince!

Misconception #10: I don't need Jesus, I need a man.

Theme: You are complete in Jesus, not half a woman.

~Roxie's story: The need for a real relationship with Jesus~

Roxie had been feeling down during the past few weeks. Her church friend, Virginia, asked what she could do to lift her spirits. They were faithful members of the church's single's ministry, but Roxie's increasing absence from the single's events caused Virginia to ask questions.

Roxie's second divorce had been final now for over three years, and the long string of lonely days and nights had begun to wear her down. She tried a couple of dates but they didn't work out. Now, she was back to square one. She painted herself as a lonely and miserable woman who would eventually grow old without the companionship of a man.

Virginia said she prayed and studied to form a plan for Roxie's situation. A few days later, Virginia called and put her plan into motion.

"Roxie," Virginia shared with her over the phone. "I want you to meet a friend of mine. He's an incredible man. Can you come over?"

"Will I like him?" Roxie questioned.

"If I were a betting woman I would bet the house on this one," Virginia assured. "Just come over as soon as you can."

"Okay," Roxie said, "just give me time to change and freshen up." Roxie hung up the phone and began dressing.

For the next twenty minutes her heart overflowed with excitement and anticipation. She carefully snuggled into her favorite outfit, arranged her hair carefully, dabbed on just the right amount of perfume, and started out to meet this incredible man. She arrived at Virginia's apartment and made sure all the parts were in the right place before ringing the doorbell. After entering the apartment her eyes cut around the room but saw no one.

"Don't tell me you let him leave." Roxie scolded.

"Hum, no, he's still here," Virginia responded. She led Roxie over to the couch. Virginia took her Bible from the table and confessed, "The man I told you about is in this book."

Disappointment gripped Roxie. "You've got to be kidding me!" She exclaimed.

Virginia gently took Roxie's hand and explained, "Roxie, I know your divorce was very difficult and the past years have been a huge challenge for you. So I wanted to share my personal testimony about the lonely moments in my life and how Jesus fulfilled all my needs. Let's read about Him together and perhaps I'll show you some things you didn't know. In other words, I want to introduce you to my man."

Roxie couldn't believe this. She was bitterly let down. She slowly rose from the couch, turned to Virginia as she opened the door and muttered, "Virginia, I know all about Jesus. I don't need Jesus. I need a man."

She slowly exited and gently closed the door.

~Whispers~

Many women know about Jesus and have been baptized, but they have never experienced His manifested presence. If you ever truly received a touch from Him, you would never be the same again. If you ever heard His voice speak to you, you would never be the same again.

If you ever felt His awesome presence, you would never be the same again. The Bible says in His presence there is fullness of joy. In other words, when you are in Christ's presence, nothing else matters. You are satisfied and at peace.

He is the only "True" and "Living God" because He is alive. He can hear, see, feel, and communicate just as other human beings can. This means women can have an intimate relationship with Him. One of the mistakes of many women is to view Christ as a historical figure only. Thus, to them, He cannot touch them or become personal in any way.

Christianity is a combination of faith and experience. But many women view it as a faith-only religion and are convinced they can never have an earthly experience with Christ.

These women may not have discovered a fulfilling relationship with Christ. But others, like Virginia, have pushed beyond the traditional barriers and developed a personal bond with Christ in such a way that they consider Him to be "their Man."

She discovered that Christ goes beyond any fantasy any woman could imagine and is the ultimate and perfect man. No human male can be Christ or fulfill your life like Christ can, but the man should constantly strive to love you as Christ loves you.

Let's look at some of the characteristics and facts about Christ that makes Him the ultimate companion.

* Christ will never abandon you.

"When my father and my mother forsake me, then the Lord will take care of me" (Psalms 27:10).

* Christ will never fall out of love with you.

"nor height nor depth, nor any other created thing, shall be able to separate us from the love of God which is in Christ Jesus our Lord" (Romans 8:39).

* Christ offers forgiveness and mercy.

"But You are God, ready to pardon, gracious and merciful, slow to anger, abundant in kindness, and did not forsake them" (Nehemiah 9:17).

* Christ offers you a fresh beginning.

"Therefore, if anyone is in Christ, he is a new creation; old things have passed away; behold, all things have become new" (2 Corinthians 5:17).

* Christ is the ultimate protection. With Him you are completely safe.

"Yea, though I walk through the valley of the shadow of death, I will fear no evil; For You are with me; Your rod and your staff, they comfort me." (Psalm 23:4)

* Christ will not withhold anything good from you.

"For the Lord God is a sun and shield; The Lord will give grace and glory; No good thing will He withhold from those who walk uprightly." (Psalm 84:11)

* Christ has rest, comfort, and peace in His arms.

"Come to Me, all you who labor and are heavy laden, and I will give you rest." (Matthew 11:28)

* Christ will not change.

"For I am the Lord, I do not change." (Malachi 3:6)

* Christ fully knows and understands you.

"O Lord, You have searched me and known me. You know my sitting down and my rising up; You understand my thought afar off." (Psalm 139:1--2)

* Christ gives you strength for the challenges of life.

"My flesh and my heart fail; But God is the strength of my heart and my portion forever." (Psalms 73:26)

* Christ gives eternal life.

"Most assuredly, I say to you, he who believes in Me has everlasting life." (John 6:47)

* In Christ you are complete. You are whole, neither lacking nor missing anything.

"For in Him (Christ) dwells all the fullness of the Godhead bodily; and you are complete in Him, who is the head of all principality and power." (Colossians 2:9-10)

When a woman discovers Christ in a living and personal way, He steps off the pages of the Bible and becomes a real person in her life. She ceases seeing Him in the traditional non-personal ways. She now becomes familiar with a living, breathing Person in Christ and experiences His comfort, strength, and unconditional love.

I must admit, I spent many years seeing Christ in religious terms only. But after our thirteen year-old son suddenly died from a rare heart disease, I found myself needing more from Christ than words on a page.

While my wife was in deep depression and I was about to drown in sorrow, I poured out my heart to Jesus in this fashion: "I believe every word of the Bible, but I need You to become real in my life. I need to hear Your voice, to feel Your touch, and to sense Your comfort and strength within me. If You truly are alive like the Bible says, then come into my life and help me."

Jesus became real in more ways than one. I had never experienced peace of that magnitude in my entire life. He comforted me in ways that only He could. At times He carried me from one day to the next. Joy and peace seemed to erupt from nowhere. His presence was unmistakably incredible.

There were times when He was so close to me I felt as though I could reach out and touch Him.

These experiences have driven me to tell the world that He's real. He's not a psychological event, a figment of my imagination, a mere historical figure, nor a religious belief. He's as real as my wife and as real as my daughter. Because He's real, He interacts with me by touching me, comforting me, strengthening me, and loving me with unconditional love.

Listen to what happened to Roxie only weeks after she left Virginia's apartment.

~End of Whispers~

Virginia didn't allow Roxie's cold response to discourage her. She continued to speak sparingly with Roxie about her personal and intimate relationship with Christ. Roxie couldn't help but notice Virginia's happiness and joy. Finally, weeks later, Roxie decided she needed what Virginia had.

Roxie washed and dressed herself up and went to Virginia's apartment. When Virginia answered the doorbell, she seemed surprised to see Roxie standing there, dressed as if she were going on a date.

"Ah, hi Roxie," Virginia managed to say. "What's this surprise visit all about?"

Roxie smiled and answered, "I decided to take you up on that offer to meet your friend."

Virginia was stunned, then answered, "Oh, that friend! You mean my man?"

"No," Roxie said—lovingly embracing her. "Our Man!"

They sat on the couch and Virginia began to share her awesome experiences with Christ. As they finished with prayer, Roxie could sense something strange happening within her soul. She went home rejoicing and soaking in the joy and peace of her newly formed relationship with Christ.

Prayer: Jesus, I need You to become real in my life. I accept You as the only True and Living God. Please forgive me of all my sins and show Yourself to me in a personal way. I pray in the name of Jesus the Christ. Amen.

Focus: If you are sincere about accepting and knowing Him, He will come into your life. You cannot try it as an experiment just to see what will happen. You must be willing to give Him your life, your love, and your whole heart!

Chapter Eleven Highlights

Many women know about Jesus and have been baptized, but they have never experienced His manifested presence. If you ever received a touch from Him, you would never be the same again.

But others like Virginia have pushed beyond the traditional barriers and developed a personal bond with Christ in such a way that they consider Him to be, "their Man."

He's not a psychological event, a figment of my imagination, a mere historical figure, nor a religious belief. He's as real as my wife and as real as my daughter. And because He's real, He interacts with me by touching me, comforting me, strengthening me, and loving me with unconditional love.

Chapter Eleven Self Evaluation Questions:

Supporting Scriptures: Psalms 139:1-6, 13-18; Col 2:9-10; Hebrews 4:14-15

Do you feel whole or missing nothing without a man?

Do you have a personal relationship with Christ?

Is Christ really first in your life or is that spot given to a man?

I can relate to this chapter because:

Chapter 12
Putting It All Together

~Deborah's ending: Back to the present in her hotel room~

~The Epiphany (The encounter with Jesus)~

As Deborah curled up in the dark quiet corner of her hotel room, she could sense the battle beginning within. She tried to block the burning occurrences of long ago that never graced the pages of her book. But a heavy sense of fear, coupled with shame and worthlessness, filled her being so much that the atmosphere of the room felt dreary.

She buried her face between her knees, tightly closed her eyes, uttered a prayer, and began to slowly rock back and forth in an attempt to comfort herself. Several minutes later, an intensely bright light appeared. She thought someone had turned on the lights, so she lifted her head to investigate. The light was so bright that it temporary blinded her.

She held her hands over her eyes and called out, "Who is it? Who's there?" No response came. But she could sense the shift in the atmosphere of the room. The heavy environment of fear, shame, and worthlessness was chased away. In its place lingered a sweet sense of peace that she had never experienced before.

Then an incredibly heavenly voice, unlike anything she had ever heard before, spoke to her and said, "Deborah, I see you."

Still unable to look directly at the light, she knew this wasn't an encounter with a human being. She managed to ask, "Who are you?" She was gripped with excitement mixed with reverential fear.

"I am the One who knows you," the Voice replied. "I see you, and I know your pain and sorrow."

With those words, Deborah knew exactly who it was. There was something about the brightness of His presence that drained her strength. Then the Voice spoke again, "Deborah, you must empty yourself of the hurt and anger."

She didn't need to ask what those words meant. She knew what she was holding back and trying furiously not to face. When the painful thoughts of the most hurtful incidents in her life began to flood her mind, she slowly stretched out face down on the floor, and wept bitterly.

She asked the Voice, "Why did You let them do that to me?" Only silence returned. She continued to cry as the images of the most terrible years of her life began to scroll through her mind.

She saw the gruesome faces of her last foster parents. She was just eleven years old when she was placed with the family. She was their only child. They seemed friendly during the first few months, but afterwards things went terribly wrong.

No matter what she did and how she did it, it was never good enough for them. They had ways of making her wish she were dead — constantly telling her she would never amount to anything and calling her names like "trash" and "ignorant." Often, as punishment for Deborah's many "crimes" as they referred to them, they locked Deborah up for hours at a time down in a dark, cold, and dreary cellar.

Deborah screamed, pleaded, promised to be good, but they still threw her in that awful place. She could still envision the total darkness around her. She could still smell the musty odor of old clothes and feel the spider webs draping over her skin.

But that wasn't the worst part. The thing she found horrible was the stone cold silence. For hours, she heard nothing but the beating of her heart and the blowing of her breath as she curled up in the fetal position—crying like there was no tomorrow. She called out--pleading with them, "Please don't do this." But they ignored her pleas.

Hours later, when they finally came to open the door, it was like coming up out of water to breathe. She struggled to catch her breath, fell at their feet, and begged for another chance to make it up to them. Things would be okay for a while, but eventually she found myself right back in that awful place, curled up, listening to the silence, and feeling as if she was about to lose her mind.

After reliving the nightmare, she sobbed, "Why did You let them do that to me? Why? Why?" She relaxed her body and began to release a flood of hurt, pain, and bitterness. As her tears flooded the floor, the Voice spoke softly, "Deborah, I love you. Do you remember what I went through for you at the cross? You went through trials for someone else."

As Deborah continued to weep, she felt a hand touch her shoulder in the gentlest way. At that very instant, comfort, peace, and a strange sense of joy overflowed her being. Her strength returned. As quickly as the light came, it disappeared. But the peaceful atmosphere that came with the light remained in the room. She continued to bathe in the sweetness of the moment.

Minutes later, she slowly rose to her feet, walked toward the window in the living room, and peered at the magnificent scenery. This time, there was no dreadful feeling, only an admiration for the beautiful reflection of the moon dancing on the water. The lake seemed to call her name.

She washed her face, threw on some clothes, grabbed a small blanket, and walked down to the lake. She sat on the bench and wrapped herself in the blanket. She slowly breathed in, smelling the misty dew. Only the sound of cricket chirps broke the silence of the night. For the first time in many years, the peace and quiet of the night didn't usher in nightmares.

She thought about the awesome event that happened earlier that night, about the words she heard, about the touch that set her free, and about the meaning of the words, "Do you remember what I went through for you at the cross?"

Then she thought about what Jesus went through for her. The shame, agony, torture, and agonizing pain of the crucifixion. All for her. She pondered, He went through hell, just for me. That's why He said He loved me. Then she began to mull over His final words before leaving, "You went through trials for someone else."

She thought about the women in her meetings and how they always found ways to empty themselves of all the grief, heartache, and anger. Now she realized why they connected to her and clung to her every word. She finally understood why Jesus allowed it to happen. It was for them. They needed someone to lead them out of the darkness into the light. They needed someone who had already been through it.

She pondered further and came to the simple conclusion, "It's not about me."

She realized those terrible things that happened to her were not all about her alone. The pain was real. The heartaches happened. But it wasn't all about her. It was about helping someone else and introducing them to Jesus Christ. She finally found complete and total peace within. She slowly inhaled, then exhaled, and closed her eyes as the gentle night breeze caressed her face.

~The next morning at the hotel~

Deborah awoke to the voice of a male hotel attendant. "Excuse me Miss, are you okay? Did you sleep out here all night?" The attendant curiously asked.

She stretched, slowly gained the focus in her eyes, and gazed around to take in the environment. She found herself sitting by the lake, still wrapped in the blanket, and that the calm night had given way to daybreak.

"Ah, I guess I must have fallen asleep out here," She explained, "I didn't mean to—it was just so incredibly calm and relaxing."

The attendant nodded, "Yeah, we have people sleeping out here pretty often. The scenery and relaxing atmosphere can certainly lull you to sleep. Are you sure you can get back into your room?"

She checked her pocket and found a room key. "Yeah, I'm okay," She whispered, "Thanks for checking on me."

"No problem Miss," he responded.

She made my way back to the room. She checked the time and discovered she was due on stage in a little over an hour. She rushed into the shower, dressed herself, and headed across the street to the convention center. The crowds were already filling the building. As she went through the side door to meet with the event managers, she could feel the early morning event would be different from all the others.

The women participated in the usual exciting events leading up to her introduction, and she stepped out on stage once more for her final ministry moments in that city.

She spoke once again about her struggles, heartaches, and trials, taking a few moments to share events recorded in her book. But then, instinctively, she stopped speaking, walked to the end of the stage, and sat on the steps facing the audience.

She breathed deeply and exhaled. She needed strength for what she was about to say. She pushed out a breath prayer, then looked into the eyes of the women who were anxiously awaiting her next words.

She confessed, "You know, I've been traveling for several years, speaking from my book, and seeing thousands of women receive emotional healing. But until last night, I had never experienced that healing myself."

Some of the women in the crowd looked puzzled and began to quietly whisper to each other.

She breathed in and out again. "I didn't come clean about some events in my life," she continued. "As a result, they had power over me and over my mind. I found out the hard way that you can't overcome what you don't admit happened. I want to share something with you that's not written in my book."

She began to tell the story of the horrid abuse and torture from her last foster parents. The audience was so quiet that at times she thought they had tuned out. But she could tell from some of their faces that they too had similar secrets lurking somewhere in the corner of their mind.

By the time she finished recalling those nights of hell on earth, there were many tear-soaked faces in the crowd. Sniffling came from all directions, tissue was shared in abundance, and weeping could be heard from many. She hesitated for a few moments, just to allow those hurting women to remember, confess, and focus on the most horrendous moments of their lives.

She spoke again, "I've asked myself many times why God allowed those horrible things to happen to me. Last night I received my answer. The Lord showed me that my life hasn't been about me."

She went on to explain how those incidents in her life would mean healing for someone else going through the same thing. She talked about the comfort, peace, and joy of Jesus Christ, and what it really means to "empty" yourself of all the hurt and pain of the past.

At the end of her conversation, one by one, women began making their way to the stage. She instructed the stage security team to allow them through. The first woman came to the stage and tearfully embraced her, whispering in her ear, "That happened to me." Within the next five minutes hundreds of weeping women surrounded her and we held onto each other for comfort. She took the microphone and began to pray, "Jesus, here we all are, broken, wounded, and weeping. We've all had very difficult and painful experiences in our lives. But You are the only Person who knows exactly how we feel, how we hurt, and how we try to keep living day by day. I thank You for loving us, for wanting us, and for healing us. Now, I only ask that You comfort us, and help us to find the peace and joy You promised. Please heal my sisters, and please give them the same peace You gave me. I pray in the marvelous name of Jesus Christ. Amen."

As she finished, she could sense the presence of Jesus, healing, comforting, and strengthening that crowd of women as they emptied themselves of all the hurt and pain. She looked around, took in the faces of those who had been touched and delivered, then looked up to heaven and said:

"Free at last."

~Whispers~

Deborah finally found healing from a broken past as well as her ultimate purpose in life. What about you? Where do you go from here?

Please don't finish reading this book, place it on your bookshelf, say to yourself, "That was a good book," and go about living the same life with no changes. This book was written to change lives like yours for the better. So where do you go from here? It all depends on where you are now. If you are:

* Having problems conquering your quiet place.

First of all, confess the issue to God and perhaps to a godly person who will give you biblical advice. You must seek forgiveness, even if it's for something you've done but have managed to overlook. After this, you are on the way to conquering your quiet place.

* Seeing yourself or life in an incorrect way.

Read the scriptures at the end of that particular chapter. Ask God to create in you a clean heart and renew within you a right spirit. You must work on change. It doesn't happen merely because you desire it. Seek out other scriptures regarding that subject matter, and meditate on them daily until change comes.

* Having issues with trust or respect regarding men.

Forgiveness must be attained. Although this can be very difficult, it is also very necessary. If you cannot achieve forgiveness, those issues of trust and disrespect will always follow your future relationships. You must be able to separate your past relationships from the present or future ones. A suggested book for reading is entitled *Forgiveness: Walk Me Through It,* authored by myself.

   * **Living your life for God only and not interested in a relationship right now.**

I applaud and respect your decision to live such a life. In fact, the apostle Paul referred to it as a gift to be able to live in celibacy. But it must not be chosen out of bitterness toward men.

Remember, you are not half a person. You are whole, missing nothing in Christ. As long as you feel complete and fulfilled without a man, you are viewing the situation properly. Continue to live your life for Christ and be a witness to the single and married women.

   * **In a relationship with a man who doesn't know Christ.**

Go to God in prayer and ask Him to lead the man in the right direction, and in the process prepare you to be a godly woman. Share some of the points in this book with him and pray for God to send someone in his life for guidance.

   * **In a relationship with a godly man.**

I applaud you and praise the Lord that you have a man who is learning how to love you as Christ loves the Church. By now you must know that even this relationship will have issues. But because Christ is leading you both, there should be forgiveness and reconciliation on the road to developing intimacy. Don't forget your responsibility to help other struggling women find what you now enjoy.

* **Wanting to know Christ in the way described in this book.**

Christ makes a promise to all who desire to become intimate with Him. He will make Himself known to them in a special way. If your heart is searching for that unique bond with Christ, just ask Him to come into your life and make Himself known. If you're really sincere, as God knows your heart, He will show Himself to you in ways you never imagined.

Just surrender your thoughts, your ways, and your mind totally to Him. And prepare yourself for the experience of your life.

~Bits of wisdom about men~

When a man does enter your life, make sure he is a man who:

* **Loves Christ and has a relationship with Him.**

Not every man in the church has a true relationship with Christ. One test is to begin a conversation about Christ. If he cuts it short, he probably doesn't have a relationship. But if he continues to talk and seems to enjoy the conversation, more than likely he does have a relationship. Christ is the only Person who can teach him how to love you.

* Respects women.

Pay attention to how he speaks and treats his mother and other females in his life. This is a good indicator of how he will treat you. Never settle for a disrespectful man no matter how bad you feel about yourself or how good you feel about him.

* Knows his role as a man.

A man cannot fulfill what he doesn't know. Sometimes he must be taught how to be a man. There is certainly a shortage of male role models today, but the Lord will provide if you ask Him to send someone into the man's life to guide him.

* Isn't rushing you into sexual relations or marriage.

It takes time to get to know a person and to build intimacy. Never allow a man to rush you into doing things you know aren't right. If he is a man of God, he will take his time to get to know you. After all, he is testing you to see if you are the person God sent to him.

~Words of encouragement~

Woman, you are incredible and unbelievable. If you only knew it and lived it out with confidence in your life.

As for now:

No more tears over a man who doesn't love you the way he should. It's his loss.

No more tears over an unfaithful man. He has the problem, not you.

No more tears over an image in the mirror. You are beautiful from the inside out.

No more tears over mistreatment by blind men who can't see your beauty.
No more tears over your past mistakes with men. Jesus gives you a fresh start.

Instead, I pray that you have:

Tears of joy when you develop an intimate relationship with Christ.

Tears of joy when Christ touches you in a special way.

Tears of joy when Christ whispers sweet nothings in your ear.

Tears of joy when Christ assures you of a future and a hope.

Tears of joy when Christ takes your hand and leads you to breath taking places.

Tears of joy when Christ fulfills your every need and every desire.

In the words of Jesus to a woman healed of a back disease:

"Woman, you are loosed from your infirmity."
(Luke 13:12)

Remember to keep Christ first, and He will teach you to be fulfilled in your earthly relationships. Now go into the world and carry out great accomplishments for your man, Jesus Christ.

Chapter Twelve Highlights

Then an incredible voice, unlike anything she heard before, spoke to her, "Deborah ...I see you."

She started speaking again. "I've asked myself many times why God allowed those horrible things to happen to me. And last night I received my answer. The Lord showed me that my life hasn't been about me."

She went on to explain how those incidents in her life would mean healing for someone else going through the same thing. She talked about the comfort, peace, and joy of Jesus Christ, and what it really means to "empty" yourself of all the hurt and pain of the past.

Chapter Twelve Self Evaluation Questions

Supporting Scriptures: John 4:13-14

Have you searched every corner of your mind for unresolved issues?

Have you confided in anyone about the most hurtful events in your life?

What are some of the points in this book that you can apply in your life?

I can relate to this chapter because:

Chapter 13

The Essence of a Woman

Theme: Understanding why you are the way you are.

I want to end this book by painting a vivid image of who you are in regards to your womanhood as it relates to your heavenly Father. I want you to see yourself clearly.

The dictionary defines the word "essence" in part as "the basic, real, and invariable nature of a thing." Some synonyms for the word essence are "substance," "character," and "attribute."

Humanly speaking, a person cannot choose their "essence"; rather it has been established for them before birth. For example, a child cannot choose their maternal parents. That choice was made before they were born, and the child's essence was determined by the parents.

In other words, the child cannot choose their DNA, their sex, their hair color, eye color, and other physical characteristics before they are born. These things are determined by the genetic makeup of the parents. In fact, the child doesn't even get to choose their name. The parents choose it for them.

Just as it is in the physical, so it is in the spiritual. You did not get to choose which characteristics the Father gave you in terms of spiritual character. These were determined before you were born. As the human genetics determine your physical composition, the genetics of your heavenly Father determine spiritual composition.

Therefore, whenever we want to understand certain things about ourselves, about our character, our passions, our desires, and our abilities, one of the places we should look for answers is our heritage.

Knowing this, let's examine some character aspects of your heavenly Father and spiritual Parent, to point out some aspects of His character that also reside within you.

1. Like your Father, you have exceptional creativity.

As I was sitting by a lake, reading and meditating on the Word of God, I noticed all the ducks that were walking along the banks and others swimming in the water. I focused on the differences in their color. Some were all white, some gray, and some gray and black with a touch of white close to their beaks. Though they all were ducks, they didn't all go in the same direction, swim at the same time, or eat at the same time. They were all ducks, but they were each unique.

Then I gazed at the trees that surrounded the lake and provided shade from the scorching midday sun. Again, though they all were trees, they were of different shapes, sizes, types, and colors.

When I peered at the entire scenery of the lake, everything seemed to blend together to form one giant snapshot of beauty. After my amazement subsided, I came to this one simple conclusion about the Father of the universe: "Lord God, You are very creative!"

As your Father is creative, so are you. The spiritual gene of creativity lies within you. It's the ability to take things that are different shapes, sizes, and colors, and creatively put them together to form a perfect picture.

I've watched with amazement as women have created stunning flower displays before my very eyes. I've often asked them, "How did you do that? How did you know those colors and sizes would be splendid together?"

They often reply with the simple answer, "I just knew."

You have an eye for creativity that was passed on to you by your heavenly Father. Not only in terms of nature, but also in terms of home life, business, spiritual matters, and other areas of your life, some of which you have yet to explore.

Some women might respond, "But I'm no good with flowers." That doesn't mean you don't have the gene of creativity. In order to be creative, you have to visualize the finished product, whether it is a flower display, a business, or another area of your life.

You have the ability to be creative with whatever your needs and desires in life happen to be. All you need to do is believe it and allow His creative genes to flow through your being. When you do this, you will create unbelievably exquisitely awesome displays that tell the world, "I am my Father's daughter."

2. Like your Father, you have an eye for beauty.

As I was driving over the mountain, I saw a sign that said, "The scenic route." Curious, I took that road. It led me up to a small parking lot nestled near the highest peak. I exited the car and stood overlooking the valley below. As I breathed in the fresh mountain air, my eyes were drawn to the fantastic colors of the trees.

There were bright colors that yelled, "Look at me!" It wasn't as if they were trying to compete against each other. Instead, they all complemented each other. The green, pink, orange, yellow, light red, and others all blended together to form a beautiful landscape.

I thought about another beautiful scene I visited sometime earlier. It was a waterfall, carved in the middle of mountains, that had different shades of greenery on both sides of the falling water. It was set against the background of a lazy blue sky and crowned with the sound of water flowing into the stream below. I remember taking in the view, the peace and quiet, the sound of rushing water, and the feel of the gentle breeze of midday. Again, I thought about the hands and mind that created these scenes and exclaimed within myself: Heavenly Father, You have an eye for beauty!

As your Father does, so do you. You have the genes to visualize and produce beautiful things. As with creativity, I'm simply amazed at the ability of women to beautify houses, businesses, offices, sanctuaries, and other places. I'm left wondering, "How did you do that? How did you know those colors, shapes, and sizes would be beautiful when blended together?"

I often get the same answer: "I just knew."

Just as your Father creates beauty, so can you. You have the spiritual gene of beautification. Not just in terms of physical appearance, but also in terms of substance.

You have the ability to raise beautiful children (respectful, kind, generous, etc). You have the ability to cultivate a beautiful marriage and beautiful relationships with family and friends. You know beauty is not just about the exterior. You have the creative ability to beautify in substance as well as in appearance. This can only be the hallmark of your heavenly Father.

3. Like your Father, you have a desire to love and be loved.

The living scriptures proclaim the first and greatest commandment is, "You shall love the Lord your God with all your heart, and with all your soul, and with all your mind" (Matthew 22:37). In the sight of our heavenly Father Himself, this is His first and greatest desire for us, that we love Him fully, with our total being. Then He emphatically shows His love for us in the scriptures: "Behold what manner of love the Father has bestowed on us, that we should be called children of God!" (1 John 3:1).

These scriptures testify that the Father both loves us with all of Himself and wants all of our love in return.

It would seem somewhat strange that a totally powerful and intelligent being as our heavenly Father, who can have anything He wants, would have love as number one on His list of desires. Not only love, but our full love. In other words, he wants our total being directed toward Himself first, then toward others second.

Woman, because you are a product of your Father, you also desire to love and to be loved fully. Of course, I am not talking about having someone love you more than they love the heavenly Father. Rather, I am simply talking about human relationships.

When you love, you have a desire to love with all you have. When you are being loved, you have the desire to be loved with all that person has. You desire a full and total commitment from any relationship you have, not just marital.

Some people call this "loving hard." I simply call it a gene given to you by the Father.

Have you ever wondered why intimate betrayal hurts you so much, why you seem to fall in love so quickly, or why you have determined what you want out of the relationship while the man is still wondering?

Ever wondered why you have such a difficult time getting over a bad relationship, why you end up going back to a man you clearly shouldn't be with? It's simply because of your desire to love and to be loved fully.

The following scripture in Matthew 23:37 indicates God's passion and desire to fully love and to be loved:

"O Jerusalem, Jerusalem, the one who kills the prophets and stones those who are sent to her! How often I wanted to gather your children together, as a hen gathers her chicks under her wings, but you were not willing."

Jesus desired to love Israel, and He wanted them to return that love with all of themselves. But they rejected Him and turned His offer of love away. So He lamented and mourned within Himself for the love that was lost.

I celebrate the gene of passion and desire for love that the Father has passed in you. Yet, please be cautious. Sometimes you can place yourself in some very difficult situations because of your desire to love and be loved. Always allow the Lord to place you in relationships of love and intimacy. When He does, you will find the true love the Father desires you to have.

4. Like your Father, you have wisdom and knowledge.

When we read the incredible account of creation in the book of Genesis, we see quite clearly the wisdom and knowledge of the Father. He created the trees and other plants on the third day, and the Sun on the fourth day because plants need sunlight.

On the sixth day the Father created animals and mankind knowing both would need plants to eat and water to drink. He never had to erase creation and start all over again. Instead, He declared everything He made was good and very good. This leads me to think about the wisdom and knowledge of our Father. The scriptures declare,

"Oh, the depth of the riches both of the wisdom and knowledge of God! How unsearchable are His judgments and His ways past finding out!" (Romans 11:33)

This aspect of the Father's character does not end with Him. He has passed the gene of wisdom and knowledge on to you. You have the ability to make wise decisions and choices about anything life has to offer.

One of the characteristics that separate you from the rest of the Father's worldly creation is your ability to reason, to weigh consequences, and formulate plans based on intelligent data and thoughts. Your most valuable earthly possession is not your body, it's your mind. It's your intellect, your ability to calculate, examine, and reach conclusions about subjects and ideas.

Therefore, as the scriptures instruct us to do, ask your Father for divine wisdom and knowledge that will help you avoid unnecessary heartaches and pain. Life is difficult enough without adding our own failures and shortcomings.

You are equipped to make wise decisions about your family, about your occupation, about your business, and about your spiritual life for the Lord. Just rest on the Father's promises found in His word and believe He has given you all you need to live in victory.

5. Like your Father, you have a sense of mystery about you.

Throughout the scriptures, your Father unmistakably displays a sense of mystery about Himself. He reveals only what others need to know at that particular time. It took over 400 years of slavery before He revealed His name, "I AM THAT I AM" to Moses.

Even that revelation is incomplete. It's only what we need to know and the rest will be revealed in perfection at the end of time. (See 1 Corinthians 13:9-11)

Please notice in the scriptures that every time the Father revealed Himself to humans, He didn't allow them to see His full being. Sometimes He appeared in a cloud, smoke, or in some other form. When He was about to appear before the nation of Israel at Mount Sinai, He warned Moses not to allow anyone, human or animal, to come near the mountain (Exodus 19:12).

Even after God descended to the mountain, shielded by smoke and fire, He again instructed Moses to go down the mountain and make sure no one tried to break through the barriers to take a look at Him.

Notice what the Father does for Moses in Exodus 33. Moses asked the Father to allow him to see His glory. In other words, Moses wanted to see the Father uncovered, without clouds, smoke, and fire obstructing the view. Because the Father had a special intimacy with Moses, He agreed to show Moses His back only—for the Father said to Moses:

"You cannot see my face: for no man shall see Me and live" (Exodus 33:20).

God hid Moses in a cliff between two rocks, passed by Moses while covering him with His hand, then removed His hand and Moses was allowed to see the back of the Creator of the galaxy, universe, and of all mankind. What excitement— what a joyous and soul stirring event it must have been.

The scriptures don't record what Moses saw. Why? Because what Moses saw was only for his eyes. Moses had the intimacy and permission to see God—but not others.

Moses is the only sinful human recorded in the Bible to see the back of the Father. In other words, the Father doesn't uncover Himself for just anyone and everybody. A person must have true intimacy with the Father before this is even possible.

To all others, there is a sense of mystery about the Father, in regards to seeing Him uncovered. All others only get to see the Father from afar. But Moses, because of his intimacy with the Father, saw a part of Him that no one else, other than Jesus, had the pleasure of looking upon.

Woman, this sense of mystery is not just meant for the Father. It's also meant for you. You should have such a sense of mystery about yourself that others often wonder things about you, particularly when it comes to your physical body. You should regard your body as your Father regards His-- holy, sacred, and only to be seen by the person who has a certain level of intimacy.

Let's be very clear here. The level of intimacy I'm referring to is the godly man who has promised to love you for better or for worse, in sickness and in health, and till death do you part. After the marriage is completed, and these final words are proclaimed, "I now pronounce you man and wife."

After marriage is when he should be allowed to "see your glory." I'm not saying to cover up from head to toe. But I am saying dress yourself properly and do not reveal parts that shouldn't be revealed.

We live in a world today that doesn't believe in holding anything back. In fact, worldly women want everyone to see everything they have. There is no sense of mystery whatsoever. They put their most of their bodies on display for the entire world to see.

Why? Because to them their bodies are their gods. They want attention and compliments from men and women. They want to be thought of highly in the minds of humans. They want to be accepted in a world that views proper dress as "old fashioned" and "dreary." The only thing that matters to them is to be labeled "beautiful" by the world.

But you, because you are your Father's daughter, should not follow their example. You should cover yourself properly so as not to show certain parts of your body that should be reserved for your husband only. Again, I'm not advocating dark covering from head to toe. But what I am saying is to avoid revealing certain parts of your "glory" for everyone to see.

In short, have an air of mystery about yourself, just like your Father has about Himself. When you do this, the honeymoon will be filled with anticipation and excitement. The marriage will have many moments of discovery that will last a lifetime.

6. Like your Father, you have an air of glory about you.

Throughout the scriptures, when the Father makes an appearance or allows someone to see into the heavenly realm, one word seems to make its way into most of those events; Glory. The scriptures declare:

"Be exalted, O God, above the heavens; Let Your glory be above all the earth" (Psalm 57:5).

That word "glory" in this context means "splendor." It can also mean the overwhelming brilliance of the Father, not just in terms of brightness, but also in terms of holiness. The Father's presence brings with it a sense of awesomeness and brilliance.

The priests in the temple during Solomon's day experienced the presence of the Father. As a result, they could not even stand to perform their duties (1Kings 8:11).

The prophet Isaiah saw the glory of the Father and thought he was doomed to die (Isaiah 6:1--5).

Peter, James, and John saw the glory of Jesus when He was transfigured on the mountain and witnessed His clothing become as white as the light (Matthew 17:1--3).

While exiled on the isle of Patmos, John saw the glory of the risen Lord and fell at the feet of Jesus as though he were dead (Revelation 1:12-17).

All these incidents are incredible indeed, but what happened to Moses when he saw the glory of the Father was truly astonishing. The face of Moses had a glow, in so much that the people stared intently upon him. Finally, Moses had to put a veil over his face when speaking to the people and uncover his face when speaking to the Father (Ex 35:28-35).

Something happened to Moses when he saw the back of the Father. The Father's glory was reflected on the face of Moses.

However, the glory of the Father is not just the expressed brightness of His presence. The source of the glory of the Father comes from His character.

His glory is awesome because He is holy, pure, gracious, slow to anger, long-suffering, kind, patient, faithful, truthful, compassionate, and many other qualities of holiness.

Yet this same awesome Father instructs you by saying: **"You shall be holy, for I the Lord Your God, am Holy."** (Leviticus 19:2)

The Father would have never told you to be holy if He knew it was impossible for you to accomplish. He has already given you the wisdom, knowledge, and desire to be holy as He is holy. As He continues to take you from glory to glory, molding and shaping you into the image of Jesus Christ, you will begin to reflect the glory of your Father.

Your face may not have a glow such as Moses, but others will notice something different about you. Not necessarily in your dress, but certainly in your character, the way you treat others, the way you forgive when wronged, and the way you love others with the love of Christ.

In fact, the Father is calling upon His daughters to come out of various places to receive and reflect His glory. He's calling women to come out of the night clubs, out of the bars, out of ungodly relationships, out of depression and anxiety, out of fear and loneliness, out of worldliness and materialism, and out of idol worship to receive and reflect the glory of the Father.

Will you answer the call? I believe with all my heart you will. After all, **you are your Father's daughter.**

Chapter 14

The Path to Dating & Marriage

My daughter made her thoughts about a certain young man known with these words, "He's hot!"

"He may be hot," I cautioned her, "but the main question happens to be, "Is he saved?"

Learning, as a young lady, to properly evaluate a young man isn't an easy task in this image conscious world. It seems everyone is constantly being presented as the next "hot" or "sexiest" man on earth. There are times when young ladies fall for the hype hook, line, and sinker.

This chapter contains wisdom about dating and marriage that will help you, as a young woman, to choose your dates and marriage partner wisely and according to scripture. Let's plunge right into the waters by addressing dating. Before dating begins, there are a series of questions that should be asked and answered about yourself.

Am I ready to Date?

Many women begin dating at a certain age, but age alone isn't enough to determine if someone is ready for dating. In my opinion, Christian women should only date Christian men. Besides this, there are several other factors that should be considered into the overall equation.

The first factor is discipline. Are you a disciplined person? Do you do what is expected of you when it needs to be done? If you're young enough to still be accountable to your parents, do you follow their instructions willingly or do they have to constantly remind and repeat things to you? If you're a mature woman, are you a disciplined person when comes to the workplace or family responsibilities? Discipline is very important because there are all types of problems that can happen during dating that only discipline can solve.

For example, it's discipline that will bring you home at the right time. It's discipline that will cause you to go to the right places and not the wrong places. It's discipline that will lead you to say "no" to ungodly offers and suggestions that he may have to offer. It's discipline that will guide you through this dating period without allowing you to wonder into areas of harm. Without discipline, many women and young girls tend to end up in wrong places, doing wrong things, and resulting in much heartache and pain.

The second factor is patience. Are you a patient person? Can you wait for certain things to happen or do you try to find ways to rush things? Do you tend to reply to others too quickly, leading to arguments and awkward moments? How do you behave in slow or stalled traffic? How do you react when you have to wait longer than expected in fast-food drive-through windows or walk-in restaurants?

Patience is very important in dating. You must have patience in order to find out the truth about a man's character. People will not show you their real character until they become completely comfortable with being around you. This takes some considerable time.

One of the things that frustrates me about young women is their quick way of giving up information. It's not uncommon for women to give out their phone number, place of residence, work information, and other pertinent data during the first meeting with a man. This is not what you should do and this is where patience will play a role. Always remember, there is a time for everything. Therefore, wait for the right time in order to do the right thing.

The third factor is self-control. We live in a society that practically screams, "We're out of control and we don't care who knows it!" You will likely meet a man that you will be very interested in getting to know. Perhaps he will have eyes that make you melt, perfect bright white teeth, the body of a Greek god, or the charm and wittiness that makes you feel like the only woman in the world. Regardless of all these things, you must keep yourself out of temptations' way.

In other words, do not allow yourself to be put into uncomfortable situations. For example, do not go to places where both of you are alone. Always stay in public places and if possible, with other people you trust. Can you name some places where you shouldn't go? Make a list of those places and make a conscious effort to stay away from them. Can you name some places and situations that are okay? Make a list of them and focus on going to those places only during your dating.

~My list of dating places~

Places I shouldn't go:

Places I should go:

~My answers to the three factors for dating~

Do I have the discipline needed for dating?

Do I have the patience needed for dating?

Do I have the self-control needed for dating?

Information I shouldn't give during our first meeting:

Information I should give during our first meeting:

 How did you do concerning the three factors we just talked about? Do you still have some work to do before dating? Do you have the three factors mastered? Whatever your answer happens to be, don't move forward with dating until you're sure the three factors are firmly in place in your life.
Who should I date?

Let's begin by giving you the only three qualifiers found in scripture. Whomever you date should be saved, not a close family member, and of the opposite sex. Those are the only three qualifiers mentioned in specifics in the bible.

What about age, race, customs, and other options when it comes to dating? Those issues should be decided by you. If you're still young enough to answer to your parents, they should have some valuable and wise input concerning each area.

There are pertinent questions related to each category. For example, as it relates to age, what age group would you feel comfortable dating? If you consider someone who is twenty years older or younger than yourself, what type of problems could that cause? As it relates to race, what race or races would you feel comfortable dating? There is nothing in the bible that suggests you need to date within your race only, so whatever you think and however you feel about such issues should be decided beforehand.

As it relates to customs, what types of customs would be harmful to your faith of Christianity? After all, you can't simply ask a person to stop performing their customary acts if they want to be with you. They can choose to give them up, but it must be their choice and not a mandate from you.

These are issues that need to talked through and worked out before dating begins so that you and your parents (if necessary) are on the same page.

Getting to Know Your Date

People often put forth their best behavior around others. This can make it very difficult to get to know the real person. How do you get past the exterior person and down to the real person? You do it with two things, time and x-ray questions.

There are some things that only time will reveal. This is why you need to be patient and not move to the next step in your relationship too quickly. Allow him time to become comfortable around you and with you. Allow yourself time to find out important things about him and about his family. Allow time for the both of you to discover your likes, dislikes, pet-peeves, and so forth. This phase of a relationship is very exciting, so don't push through it too quickly. Take your time and enjoy it.

X-ray questions are those that are designed to reveal a person's inner-most thoughts and beliefs. These questions allow you to cut past the outer layer of casual conversation and get into the important issues in a person's life.

Here is a list of example X-ray questions to ask your date: If you're saved, what does Jesus mean to you? What is your relationship with your parents like? What types of things cause you to become angry? What types of things cause you to be happy? What dreams and plans do you have for your future?

These are all questions that require careful thought and multiple word responses. In other words, he can't just give you one-word answers like "yea", "no", or "maybe." Men are famous for giving short answers, but you shouldn't want short answers. You should want him to talk about things that are important to you in order to find things that are compatible with you. You shouldn't ask him all of the above questions at the same time. Spread them out over several periods of dating so he won't feel like you're grilling him or trying to measure him up as a potential marriage candidate.

Keep the Dating Godly

You should look at dating as the preparation ground for marriage. Therefore, as you're dating, do not give into the temptation to do ungodly things like having sex, going to ungodly places, or following him into using drugs or alcohol. In fact, if he is pressing you into these things or involved in them himself, it's time to break off the relationship.

There are guys who will say they are Christian just to go out with you, but we know actions speak louder than words. If a person's actions are consistently not those becoming of Christ, more than likely they aren't Christian.

In order to avoid any misunderstandings, you should tell him upfront that you are saving yourself for marriage and that you do not drink or use drugs. That way you both will be on one accord concerning those issues. Don't be afraid of him leaving if you tell him the truth. If he does stop seeing you, then you will know his real intentions. If his intentions weren't honorable, it's best that you know it now rather than later on down the road.

~Path to Marriage~

Let's pretend you've followed the path to dating and are approaching year three with your date. You both are getting along very well and you think he may ask you to marry him in the near future. Now is the time to ponder and answer a few very important questions.

Am I Ready for Marriage?

Do you have the necessary spiritual maturity to share your life with someone? Do you practice forgiveness toward others? This is very important because he will certainly hurt you in some way during the marriage, and you must be able to forgive and move on without holding grudges.

Are you ready to share your personal information with someone else? In a marriage, you will need to know each others' social security numbers and other private information. Are you prepared to share this with him?

Are you ready to adjust your lifestyle to include another person? When you are single, you can come and go, spend and buy, and give and take as you please. When the marriage comes mostly everything will be a negotiation. Are you prepared for that?

Do you get along with his family, in particular, his parents? This will be very important to your relationship with him. Disgruntled in-laws can make a marriage very difficult, especially if grandchildren are involved.

Will both of your incomes cover expected expenses? Love is a great thing, but it doesn't put food on the table. If there isn't food on the table, clothes for the kids, and other necessities, the strain on the marriage may be too much to bare.

Are you healed and restored from a previous break-up? If not, you may need some additional time to sort through those issues before committing to marry him.

Has he been faithful to you during your dating experience? Please don't marry a person who is actively cheating on you while you're dating. Many women expect marriage to change a man but it won't. Marriage alone doesn't change people. People must choose to change and plot a course for that change. Therefore, a dating cheater will only become a married cheater.

If you answered these questions and determined you're ready, the last thing you need to do is understand what the wedding vows mean. These vows aren't made to the man. They are made by you to God Himself. During the wedding, you are promising God that you will perform certain things toward your husband as the blessing of God covers you both.

With this in mind, it pays to understand what the vows mean. Let's go through them.

"Will you have this man to be your wedded husband, to live together after God's ordinance in the holy estate of matrimony?

Do you want this man to be your husband and will you both live your lives according to God's rules and regulations spelled out in the Holy Bible? This means that the word of God should be the highest law in your home and your children should be taught to live by it.

"Will you love him, comfort him, honor and keep him in sickness and in health; and forsaking all others, keep yourself only unto him, so long as you both shall live?"

These questions should not be taken lightly. You will promise to love him, and that love will go far beyond physical contact. You must love him when he's wrong, when he doesn't respect you, and in many other "not so loving" situations. In order to love at all times, you must commit acts of love toward him no matter how you feel about his shortcomings and failures.

You must comfort him, honor him, and take care of him. You must forsake all others, or promise to be faithful to him by not cheating or having an affair. This includes looking at another man lustfully. Remember that Jesus said if we look at another person to lust after them, we have committed adultery in our hearts. This faithfulness to him should continue throughout your lifetime.

"I take you to be my wedded husband, to have and to hold from this day forward, for better or for worse, for richer or for poorer, in sickness and in health, to love and to cherish, till death do us part according to God's holy ordinance."

You will now make a very serious vow to God, not to humans. You will vow to accept your husband and be his wife through the good times and the bad. And you will promise to continue this until one of you passes away.

Wow! These are some very serious and holy vows to make before the God of heaven and earth. Yet so many people find themselves merely repeating words during a ceremony. I believe this is part of the reason for the extremely high divorce rates of today.

I believe if you really took the time to read and study the vows beforehand, that you will be able to determine if you're ready for such a heavy commitment to a man, and most of all, to God.

Life is too precious and short lived for you to spend valuable years with a person who is not your soul-mate. That's why I believe if you follow the path to dating and the path to marriage written in this book, God will lead you, bless you, and place you in the arms of someone chosen just for you.

Have a wonderful, peaceful, and joyful time searching for the one God has for you. Remember, your Father will always be with you through any mountains and valleys you may encounter in life. God bless you my daughter.

 Minister Charles L. Holley was born in extreme poverty as the youngest of ten children, excelled to graduate from college and attained a Masters Degree. He overcame personal tragedy with the sudden death of his teenage son, launched a godly ministry, and is the author of several inspirational books.

Charlie has a special gift to minister to multiple groups—youths, adults, men, and women. His story of growing up in the deep south is one of perseverance, determination, and faith.

Born in Alabama the son of a sharecropper and maid, the youngest of ten children, he spent his early years chopping cotton, picking strawberries, and raising farm animals.

Charlie earned a B.S. in Business Administration and a Master of Biblical Counseling. He has a beautiful wife of over twenty-five years and is the father of two children—a beautiful daughter and a son who tragically died in 2001 at the age of thirteen.

Charlie loves to write books that encourage, inspire, challenge, and change the life of the reader for the better. With a powerful gift of communication and the ability to connect with the reader, he continues to speak soul-stirring inspiration to others and to write life changing books. He is a dynamic speaker who promotes his books nationally and internationally.

Visit SpeakerHolley.com for more info.

Other Books by CL Holley:

Soar Above the Pain

7 Needs of High Performing Employees

Inspirations from the Scriptures

The Next Level Forgiver

Made in the USA
Columbia, SC
11 July 2025

60329045R00089